Trash

ANDY MULLIGAN

OXFORD
UNIVERSITY PRESS

Great Clarendon Street, Oxford OX2 6DP

Oxford University Press is a department of the University of Oxford.
It furthers the University's objective of excellence in research,
scholarship, and education by publishing worldwide in

Oxford   New York
Auckland   Cape Town   Dar es Salaam   Hong Kong   Karachi
Kuala Lumpur   Madrid   Melbourne   Mexico City   Nairobi
New Delhi   Shanghai   Taipei   Toronto

With offices in
Argentina   Austria   Brazil   Chile   Czech Republic   France   Greece
Guatemala   Hungary   Italy   Japan   Poland   Portugal   Singapore
South Korea   Switzerland   Thailand   Turkey   Ukraine   Vietnam

Oxford is a registered trade mark of Oxford University Press
in the UK and in certain other countries

Database right Oxford University Press (maker)

First published in Great Britain by David Fickling Books, a division of
Random House Children's books, a Random House Group company

This educational edition first published in 2012

Published by arrangement with Random House Children's Books, one part of
the Random House Group Ltd.

British Library Cataloguing in Publication Data

Data available
ISBN: 978-0-19-913716-9
10 9 8 7 6 5 4 3
Printed by Printplus, China

PART ONE

1

My name is Raphael Fernández and I am a dumpsite boy.

People say to me, 'I guess you just never know what you'll find, sifting through rubbish! Today could be your lucky day.' I say to them, 'Friend, I think I know what I find.' And I know what everyone finds, because I know what we've been finding for all the years I've been working, which is eleven years. It's the one word: *stuppa*, which means – and I'm sorry if I offend – it's our word for human muck. I don't want to upset anyone, that's not my business here. But there's a lot of things hard to come by in our sweet city, and one of the things too many people don't have is toilets and running water. So when they have to go, they do it where they can. Most of those people live in boxes, and the boxes are stacked up tall and high. So, when you use the toilet, you do it on a piece of paper, and you wrap it up and put it in the trash. The trash bags come together. All over the city, trash bags get loaded onto carts, and from carts onto trucks or even trains – you'd be amazed at how much trash this city makes. Piles and piles of it, and it all ends up here with us. The trucks and trains never stop, and nor do we. Crawl and crawl, and sort and sort.

It's a place they call Behala, and it's rubbish-town. Three years ago it was Smoky Mountain, but Smoky Mountain got so bad they closed it down and shifted us along the road. The piles stack up – and I mean Himalayas: you could climb for ever, and many people do . . . up and down, into the valleys. The mountains go right from the docks to the marshes, one whole long world of steaming trash. I am one of the rubbish boys, picking through the stuff this city throws away.

'But you must find interesting things?' someone said to me. 'Sometimes, no?'

We get visitors, you see. It's mainly foreigners visiting the Mission School, which they set up years ago and just about stays open. I always smile, and I say, 'Sometimes, sir! Sometimes, ma'am!'

What I really mean is, *No, never – because what we mainly find is stupp.*

'What you got there?' I say to Gardo.

'What d'you think, boy?' says Gardo.

And I know. The interesting parcel that looked like something nice wrapped up? What a surprise! It's stupp, and Gardo's picking his way on, wiping his hands on his shirt and hoping to find something we can sell. All day, sun or rain, over the hills we go.

You want to come see? Well, you can smell Behala long before you see it. It must be about two hundred football pitches big, or maybe a thousand basketball

4

courts – I don't know: it seems to go on for ever. Nor do I know how much of it is stupp, but on a bad day it seems like most of it, and to spend your life wading through it, breathing it, sleeping beside it – well . . . maybe one day you'll find 'something nice'. Oh yes.

Then one day I did.

I was a trash boy since I was old enough to move without help and pick things up. That was what? – three years old, and I was sorting.

Let me tell you what we're looking for.

Plastic, because plastic can be turned into cash, fast – by the kilo. White plastic is best, and that goes in one pile; blue in the next.

Paper, if it's white and clean – that means if we can clean it and dry it. Cardboard also.

Tin cans – anything metal. Glass, if it's a bottle. Cloth or rags of any kind – that means the occasional T-shirt, a pair of pants, a bit of sack that wrapped something up. The kids round here, half the stuff we wear is what we found, but most we pile up, weigh and sell. You should see me, dressed to kill. I wear a pair of hacked-off jeans and a too-big T-shirt that I can roll up onto my head when the sun gets bad. I don't wear shoes – one, because I don't have any, and two, because you need to feel with your feet. The Mission School had a big push on getting us boots, but most of the kids sold them on.

The trash is soft, and our feet are hard as hooves.

Rubber is good. Just last week we got a freak delivery of old tyres from somewhere. Snapped up in minutes, they were, the men getting in first and driving us off. A half-good tyre can fetch half a dollar, and a dead tyre holds down the roof of your house. We get the fast food too, and that's a little business in itself. It doesn't come near me and Gardo, it goes down the far end, and about a hundred kids sort out the straws, the cups and the chicken bones. Everything turned, cleaned and bagged up – cycled down to the weighers, weighed and sold. Onto the trucks that take it back to the city, round it goes. On a good day I'll make two hundred pesos. On a bad, maybe fifty? So you live day to day and hope you don't get sick. Your life is the hook you carry, there in your hand, turning the trash.

'What's that you got, Gardo?'

'Stupp. What about you?'

Turn over the paper. 'Stupp.'

I have to say, though: I'm a trash boy with shorts. I work with Gardo most of the time, and between us we move fast. Some of the little kids and the old people just poke and poke, like everything's got to be turned over – but among the stupp, I can pull out the paper and plastic fast, so I don't do so bad. Gardo's my partner, and we always work together. He looks after me.

2

So where do we start?

My unlucky-lucky day, the day the world turned upside down? That was a Thursday. Me and Gardo were up by one of the crane-belts. These things are huge, on twelve big wheels that go up and down the hills. They take in the trash and push it up so high you can hardly see it, then tip it out again. They handle the new stuff, and you're not supposed to work there because it's dangerous. You're working under the trash as it's raining down, and the guards try to get you away. But if you want to be first in line – if you can't get right inside the truck, and that is *very* dangerous: I knew a boy lost an arm that way – then it's worth going up by the belt. The trucks unload, the bulldozers roll it all to the belts, and up it comes to you, sitting at the top of the mountain.

That's where we are, with a view of the sea.

Gardo's fourteen, same as me. He's thin as a whip, with long arms. He was born seven hours ahead of me, onto the same sheet, so people say. He's not my brother but he might as well be, because he always knows what I'm thinking, feeling – even what I'm about to say. The fact that he's older means he pushes me around now and then, tells me what to do, and most of the time I let him. People say he's too serious, a boy without a smile, and he says, 'So show me something to smile at.' He can be mean, it's true – but then again he's taken more beatings than me so maybe he's grown up faster. One thing I know is I'd want him on my side, always.

We were working together, and the bags were coming down – some of them already torn, some of them not – and that's when I found a 'special'. A special is a bag of trash, unsplit, from a rich area, and you always keep your eyes wide for one of them. I can remember even now what we got. Cigarette carton, with a cigarette inside – that's a bonus. A zucchini that was fresh enough for stew, and then a load of beaten-up tin cans. A pen, probably no good, and pens are easy to come by, and some dry papers I could stick straight in my sack – then trash and trash, like old food and a broken mirror or something, and then, falling into my hand . . . I know I said you don't find interesting things, but, OK – once in your life . . .

It fell into my hand: a small leather bag, zipped up tight and covered in coffee-grounds. Unzipping it, I found a wallet. Next to that, a folded-up map – and inside the map, a key. Gardo came right over, and we squatted there together, up on the hill. My fingers were trembling, because the wallet was fat. There were eleven hundred pesos inside, and that – let me tell you – is good money.

A chicken costs one-eighty, a beer is fifteen. One hour in the video hall, twenty-five.

I sat there laughing and saying a prayer. Gardo was punching me, and I don't mind telling you, we almost danced. I gave him five hundred, which was fair because I was the one who found it. Six hundred left for me. We looked to see what else there was, but it was just a few old papers, photos, and – interesting . . . an ID card. A little battered and creased, but you could make him out easy enough. A man, staring up at us, right into the camera, with those frightened eyes you always have when the camera flashes. Name? José Angelico. Age? Thirty-three years old, employed as a houseboy. Unmarried and living out somewhere called Green Hills – not a rich man, and that makes you sad. But what do you do? Find him in the city and say, 'Mr Angelico, sir – we'd like to return your property'?

Two little photos of a girl in school dress. Hard to say how old, but I reckoned seven or eight, with long dark hair and beautiful eyes. Serious face, like Gardo's – as if no one had told her to smile.

We looked at the key then. It had a little tag made of yellow plastic. There was a number on both sides: 101.

The map was just a map of the city.

I took it all away and slipped it down my shorts – then we kept on sorting. You don't want to draw attention to yourself, or you can lose what you find. But I was excited.

We were both excited, and we were right to be, because that bag changed everything. A long time later I would think to myself: *Everyone needs a key.*

With the right key, you can bust the door wide open. Because nobody's going to open it for you.

3

Raphael still!

I'll hand on to Gardo after this – after the evening.

You see, just after dark I realized I had something very, very, very important, because the police arrived and asked for it back.

You don't see many police in Behala, because in a shanty you sort out your own problems. There's not a lot to steal, and we don't usually steal from each other – though it happens. We had a murder a few months ago, and the police came then. An old man killed his wife – slit her throat and left her bleeding down the walls to the shack underneath. By the time they came he'd run and we never heard whether they got him. We had four police cars come on an election visit, surrounding a man who wanted to be mayor – lights flashing and radios crackling away, because they all love a show, these police. Otherwise, they have better things to do.

This time it was five men, one of them looking very important, like a senior officer – older man, fatter man. More of a boxer, with a smashed-up nose, no hair, and a mean look.

The sun had gone down. There was a cooking fire,

where my auntie was boiling up the rice, and tonight – on account of the money I'd found – we were having that precious one-eighty chicken. About thirty of us were gathered – not all to eat one chicken! That was just for the family. But it's hot in the evenings, so people are out squatting, standing, roaming.

I think Gardo had a ball and we'd been fooling around under the hoop. Now we all stood still in the headlights of this big black four-wheel-drive, and the men got out.

The boxer cop had a quick chat with Thomas, who's the main man in our little patch, and then he was talking to all of us.

'A friend of ours has a problem,' he said. Voice like a megaphone. 'It's a pretty big problem, and we're hoping you can help. Fact is, he's lost something important. We're giving good money to anyone who finds it. Another fact is, if anyone here finds it, we're going to give a thousand pesos to every family in Behala, you understand? That is how important it is to our friend. And we're giving ten thou to you – to the one who actually puts it in my hand.'

'What have you lost?' said a man.

'We've lost . . . a bag,' said the policeman, and my skin went dry and cold, but I managed not to show it. He turned and took something from the man behind him, and held it up. It was a handbag made of black plastic, big as my hand. 'It probably looks like this,' he said. 'Bit bigger, bit smaller – not exactly the same, but similar.

12

We think this bag might have something important in it that's going to help us solve a crime.'

'When did you lose it?' said someone.

'Last night,' said the policeman. 'It was put in the trash by mistake. Out on McKinley Hill, somewhere round there. And the truck picked up all the McKinley trash this morning. That means it's either here right now, or coming in tomorrow.' He watched us, and we watched him.

'Has anyone found a bag?'

I could feel Gardo's eyes fixed on me.

I so nearly raised my hand. I so nearly spoke up then and there, because ten thousand is good money. And a thousand to every family? That's what they were promising, and if they gave it, oh my! I'd be the most popular boy in the neighbourhood. But I didn't, because I was also thinking fast, thinking that I could as well give it up in the morning as now. I better be clear: I'd never had any trouble with the police before then, so it wasn't that I didn't like them or didn't want to be helpful. But everyone knows not to trust too far. What if they just took it and drove off laughing? What was I going to do to stop them? I needed time to think, so I stood there, dumb. Maybe there was a bit of calculation going on as well. If they had money to give away, then they could be raised up over ten, and we could get it all up front. If it was precious enough for them to come all this way out to see us, then perhaps ten thousand would turn into twenty?

My auntie said, 'Raphael found something, sir.'

She nodded, and all the police were looking straight at me.

'What did you find?' said the boss.

'I didn't find a bag, sir,' I said.

'What did you find?'

'I found a . . . shoe.'

Somebody laughed.

'What kind of shoe? One shoe? When was this?'

'One shoe, sir – just a lady's shoe. I can get it – it's in my house.'

'What makes you think we're going to be interested in that? You playing games?'

He was looking back at my auntie, and her eyes were back on the rice, then on me, then on the rice.

'He said he found something,' she said. 'He never said what he found. Just trying to be helpful, sir.'

The cop in charge spoke loudly. 'Listen. We're going to be back here in the morning,' he said. 'We are going to pay anyone who wants work. One day, one week – however long it takes. We need to find that bag, and we'll pay to find it.'

One of the other policemen walked over to me, quite a young man. Gardo was right next to me then, and the policeman put his hand under my chin and tilted my head up. I looked into his eyes, trying so hard not to look scared. He was smiling, but I was glad to feel Gardo right up against me, and I smiled back as best I could.

'What's your name?' he said.

I told him.

'Brothers? Sisters? This your brother?'

'My best friend, sir. This is Gardo.'

'Where do you live, son?'

I told him everything, fast and happy, smiling hard – and I watched him fix our house in his mind, and then fix my face. He rubbed my ear gently, like I was a kid. He said: 'You gonna help us tomorrow, Raphael? How old are you?'

'Fourteen, sir.' I know I look younger.

'Where's your father?'

'No father, sir.'

'That was your ma?'

'Auntie.'

'You want work, Raphael? You gonna help?'

'Sure,' I said. 'How much are you paying? I'll work for ever!' I made my smile bigger and my eyes wider, trying just to be an excited, harmless, cute little trash boy.

'One hundred,' he said. 'One hundred for the day, but if you find that bag . . .'

'I wanna help too,' said Gardo, pretending to be eight years old and showing his teeth. 'What's in the bag, sir? More money?'

'Bits and pieces. Nothing valuable, but—'

'What kind of crime?' I said. 'How's it gonna help you solve a crime? Is it a murder?'

The policeman smiled at me some more. He looked at Gardo too. 'I don't even think it will,' he said. 'But we got to give it our best shot.' He was looking at me hard again, and Gardo's arm was right round me. 'I'll see you tomorrow.'

Then the policemen climbed back into their car and drove on, and we made sure we stood right up close to show we weren't afraid, and we made sure we ran with the car and waved. Now, Behala's full of little neighbourhoods just like ours. The shacks we live in grow up out of the trash piles, bamboo and string, piled upwards – it's like little villages in amongst the hills. We watched the car, rocking over the ruts and holes, the lights going up and down. If they wanted to talk to everyone, they'd have to make the same speech ten times.

Later on, my auntie came close and said, 'Why are you telling lies, Raphael Fernández?'

'I found a wallet,' I said. 'I gave you what I found – why did you say that to them?'

She came close and she spoke quietly. 'You found the bag, didn't you? You tell me now.'

'No,' I said. 'I found money.'

'Why did you say a shoe? Why did you not tell the truth?'

I shrugged, and tried to be sly. 'Ma, I thought they might want the wallet back,' I said.

'Money in a wallet? Where's the wallet now?'

'I'm going to get it! I just didn't want to speak up in front of everyone, everyone looking right at me, and—'

'You found the wallet in a bag? You can't lie to me.'

'No!' I said. 'No.'

She looked at me hard again, and shook her head. 'You gonna get us into a lot of trouble, I think. Whose wallet was it? People always have a name, and if you—'

'I just took the money,' I said. 'I'll throw the damn thing away right now.'

'You give it to the police.'

'Why? It's not what they're looking for, Ma. I didn't find a bag.'

'Oh, boy,' she said. 'Raphael. What I'm thinking is, if they're throwing money around to get that something back, you don't want to be caught messing about with it. I am serious, Raphael. If you found anything like the thing they're wanting, you need to give it up – first thing in the morning, when they're back.'

Gardo ate with us. He often did, just as I often ate with him and his uncle. I spent the night at his, just as he spent the night at ours – I'd wake up forgetting which place I was in and who was under the blanket with me. Anyway, just as we finished, the police car came back, big and black, and drove right out of the gates.

We watched it go.

I couldn't believe Auntie had said what she said. I knew she'd had problems with the police before, on account of my father, and I guess she had some feeling, even then, that things were going to get complicated. I think she wanted to stop it all there, all at once – but I still say she was wrong. It was one of the things that made leaving easier.

I went up to my house, Gardo following. We live high, compared to many. Two rooms built out of truck pallets, with plastic and canvas holding it fast, and it's stacked over three families below. You go up three stepladders to get to it. First, the bit where Auntie and my half-sister sleep, and beyond that's another little box, about the size of a sheet. That's where me and my cousins go, and Gardo too when he's with us. My cousins were in there now, snoring away, and all around was the noise of neighbours' chatter and laughter, and radios, and someone calling.

I moved one of the cousins along, and we got close in to the side, where I store my things. It's a crate that beer came in, and it's up on one side. I've got a spare pair of shorts, another two T-shirts and a pair of slippers. I've also got my little spread of treasures, like all the boys do. With me it's a penknife I found, with a broken blade – still a good little tool. I've got a cup with a picture of the Virgin Mary. I've got a watch that doesn't go. I've got a little plastic duck, which the cousins play with, and I've got one pair of jeans. The jeans were wrapping up the precious bag, and it felt dangerous just to be unwrapping it.

Gardo held a candle close and sat hunched, watching me. We were both bending over it. When I glanced up at him, his lips were thin. The whites of his eyes stood out like a pair of eggs.

'We gotta move it,' he said. 'You can't leave it here, boy.'

'I think you're right,' I said. 'Where to?'

He paused.

I pulled out the ID and looked at the man. José Angelico, looking back at me sadly. And his little girl, more serious. 'What do you think he's done?' I said.

'Something bad,' said Gardo. 'And when they come back, I think they going to talk to you again . . . You see the way that guy was looking at you?'

I nodded.

'You see the way he was touching you? He's got you fixed.'

'I know,' I said. 'You too, maybe.' I laughed. 'You think he wants to be our special friend?'

'This isn't funny,' said Gardo. 'We need Rat.'

'Why Rat?'

'I'm thinking it's about the only place they're not gonna look.'

'You think he'll take it, though? Rat's not stupid.'

'Give him ten, he'll take it. Break his arms if he doesn't.' Gardo took the ID and put it away. 'They won't go down there, the police – they won't even see him.'

I knew it was a good plan. I knew it was the only plan as well, because we had to get it out of the house.

'Do it now?' I said.

Gardo nodded.

'Don't threaten him, though,' I said. 'He'll do it for me.'

4

Still Raphael.

So sorry, but I want to tell about Rat, and then I will hand over.

Rat is a boy – three or four years younger than me. His real name is Jun-Jun. Nobody called him that, though, because he lived with the rats and had come to look like one. He was the only kid in Behala that I knew of who had no family at all, and at that time I didn't know too much about his past. There were plenty of boys without fathers, and a lot like me without mothers either. But if you had no parents, you had aunties or uncles, or older brothers, or cousins, and so there was always somebody who would take care of you and give you a bit of the mat to sleep on, and a plate of rice. The thing about Rat was, he had nobody, because he'd come from some place way out of the city – and if it hadn't been for the Mission School he'd have been dead.

Gardo and I went back down the ladders with the candles. I'd put the bag under my T-shirt, and tried to hold my arms so it wasn't too obvious – but it was as if people didn't want to see me anyway. Auntie especially was looking away, and shifted so she had her back to us both. We crossed the roadway and were soon deep in amongst the trash.

I better say, the trash is alive at night: that's when the rats come out strong. During the day you don't see so many, and they stay out of your path. You get a surprise now and then when one jumps up, and sometimes you get a good kick and send one spinning. Not often, though. They're quick, and they can dive, jump, fly and squirm their way out of anywhere.

I followed Gardo, and on either side I was aware of the little grey movements. There is light over Behala, because some of the trucks come at night – they've rigged up big floodlights, and they're usually on. We'd gone left, right, over the little canal that just about gets through, stinking of the dead – and then off we went into a lane only the trash people use – no trucks, and not even many people. It was dead trash underfoot, and it was damp – you were up to your knees. Soon we came to one of the old belt-machines, but this one was disused and rotting. The belt itself had been stripped out, and the wooden panels had been taken. It was just a huge metal frame, rusting away. The arm that held the belt pointed up into the sky like a big finger, and now and then kids would climb it and sit in the breeze. At ground level, its legs were sunk into concrete piles, and underneath the legs was a hole.

I suppose machinery must have been down there at one time, because there were steps down, and they were slimy. Trash is often wet, and the juices are always running. Maybe the ground here was a bit lower, I don't know – but it was always muddy.

We stopped at the top of the steps, and I called out: 'Rat!'

I called quite soft – I didn't want anyone to know what we were doing, or where we were. The problem was, the kid couldn't hear me if he was down there, and I was pretty sure he would be. Where else would he be?

'Hey, Rat!' I called again. I could hear the little cheeps and squeaks. Gardo was following me now, because even though he's braver than me and stronger, he's not easy with rats. I'll kill one with my foot, but Gardo got bitten badly a while ago, and his whole hand went bad. He'll kill them, but he'd rather stay away from them. I was halfway down the steps, and a little one streaked up past me, then another.

'Rat!' I called, and my voice echoed in the machine-chamber. I got down low with the candle, trying not to breathe too deep because of the stink – and I heard him turn in his bed.

'What?' he said. He's got a high little voice. 'Who is that?'

'Raphael and Gardo. We got a favour to ask you. Can we come in?'

'Yes.'

It might seem crazy asking a kid if you can come

into his hole, but this hole was about the only thing Rat had, apart from what he wore. I would not have lived there – anywhere would have been better. For a start it was damp and dark. For another thing, I would have been scared that the trash above would fall and pile up down the stairs, trapping me, like it did on Smoky Mountain. These mountains do move. It's not us climbing about on them that makes them fall, it's usually just their own weight as the belts pile more and more stuff on. You can get caught in a fall, and it's heavy stuff. I've never known anyone killed, but one kid broke bones, falling badly. When Smoky went down, there were nearly a hundred killed, and everyone knows some of those poor souls are still down there, down with the trash, turned into trash, rotting with the trash.

Anyway, I got to the last step, trying not to think of all that, and put my candle low. There was a sudden flicker of black, and another rat – this one big as they come – shot past me, right over my shoulder.

The kid was sitting up, just in his shorts, gazing at me with frightened eyes and his big broken teeth sticking out of his mouth.

'Raphael?' he said. 'What do you want?'

I thought, I should have brought him a bit of food. He goes hungrier than most, and his face is pinched. Kids used to call him Monkey Boy before Rat, because his face does have that wide-eyed, staring look that little monkeys have. He was sitting on some layers of cardboard, and around him there were piles of rubbish that he must have been sorting. The walls and ceiling were damp brick, and there were cracks everywhere. That was where the rats came in and out, and I guessed there were nests just the other side. He had arms skinny as pencils, and Garda's crack about breaking them had made me smile. You could break Jun's arms with your finger and thumb. He was a spider, not a rat.

'We need your help,' I said.

'That's OK.'

'You don't know what we want,' said Gardo. 'How's it OK already?'

'It's OK.' The boy smiled, and his teeth gleamed out crookedly. He blinked. He has a twitch, and when he's scared, his whole head starts to shake. He wasn't scared right now, though – he was more interested. Also, I know he liked me. I wouldn't say he and I were friends, not at all. But I didn't mind working next to him, which meant we'd talk a bit, and I'd listen to his chit-chat-singing. A lot of kids would just throw things at him and laugh.

I sat down, but Gardo stayed on the step, squatting. 'You gotta hide something,' I said. I put the bag on the cardboard, and put my candle next to it. He found another and lit it, and all three of us sat in silence.

'OK,' he said. 'What's in it? Who's it belong to?' He had a thin, breathy little voice like he was six years old.

I opened the flap and unzipped it. I took out the items and laid them down. The wallet. The key. The map.

'You happy to hide it? You didn't hear the police come, did you?'

'I didn't see any police,' said Rat. 'But I can hide it if you want. See that brick? That comes right out, and the next one too. Won't last long, though – it's gonna get eaten, OK?'

'Wait,' said Gardo. 'I'm thinking about this. It's not the bag they want, is it? It's what's in the bag.'

'We've still got to hide it,' I said.

'Why don't we just sling it?'

'If we sling it,' I said, 'and they find it . . . then they'll know someone's got what's inside, maybe. If they know what they're looking for.'

'Who's looking?' said Rat. 'What did the police want?'

I told him quickly, and his eyes widened. 'Ten thousand, Raphael!' he said. 'You're crazy! Give it in and get the cash.'

'Oh yes,' said Gardo, sneering. 'You really think they'll give it? You taken in by that? And if they do, boy – you think he'll hold onto ten thousand?'

Rat looked from me to Gardo and back again.

'Look,' I said. 'We've got to hide it. They come back tomorrow – they say they're going to pay everyone to work. We all get a few days' work, maybe – give it up next week.'

26

'Everyone's happy,' said Rat. 'That's a good idea, maybe. But you got to ask, why do they want it so bad, OK? How much was in this?' His thin fingers opened the wallet and pulled out the ID card.

'Eleven hundred,' I said.

He smiled right at me. 'Anything for using my house?'

'I'll give you fifty,' I said, and he grinned even wider and touched my arm.

'You promise, OK? That's a promise?'

'Promise.'

His hands went to the map. 'We ought to find out what they want,' he said. 'What is this – buried treasure?'

'There's nothing on it,' I said. 'It's just a city map.'

He looked harder at the ID then, staring at the photograph. 'Who is this?'

'José Angelico,' I said.

I knew Rat couldn't read. He turned the paper over and over, looking at the face.

'José Angelico,' he said slowly. 'You think the police want him? You think he's a wanted man? He looks nice enough. This his little girl?'

He was looking at the child, putting the faces next to each other.

'Maybe,' I said. 'I don't know.'

'He's rich enough to send her to school,' said Rat. 'That's a school dress.'

'What if he's been murdered?' said Gardo. 'Maybe they're looking for his body – looking for the murderers too. This could be part of something bad.'

'Who lost the bag, though?' I said. 'How do you lose a bag in the trash?'

'Not by accident,' said Rat. He was staring at the photos again. 'We ought to find out who he is, OK? He might give more than the police.'

'And what's the key?' said Gardo, pointing to it. 'That's his house key, maybe. Maybe he's locked out of his house? Find out where he lives—'

'Oh no, that's not a house key,' said Rat, staring. He hadn't noticed the key in the darkness. Now he picked it up and put it next to my candle. He looked up at me again. 'Oh, my. You don't know what that is, do you?'

'Could be to a safe,' I said. 'What is it, a padlock key? What's the one-oh-one?'

'You don't know what that is!' said Rat slowly. He was teasing us. 'I do. I'll raise you to a hundred.'

'What?'

He was smiling wider than I'd ever seen him smile, and his broken teeth stuck out like straws. 'I've seen these so many times, OK – I can tell you exactly what it is and where it is. You give me that fifty? Now? Make it a hundred, or you get no further.'

'You know what it is? Really?'

Rat nodded.

I pulled out some notes, and counted them out on the cardboard. There was a skittering of feet behind the wall, and I heard somthing running right round the little room, surrounding us. There were squeakings again: the place was alive. Gardo and I sat on, looking at Rat, waiting for his great piece of information.

'Central Station,' he said softly. 'I lived there nearly a year, when I came in first of all. I can tell you for sure: this is a locker key for the left luggage. Just outside platform four, last block on the right. One-oh-one's small, up at the top – the cheapest they do. This man's left something there.'

He smiled again and we sat there, just looking at each other. Gardo whistled, and I felt my heart beat faster and faster.

'You wanna go there?' said Rat. 'We go there now if you want.'

5

Gardo here, and I take the story on from Raphael.

We agreed to split the story because some things he forgets – like he wanted to go to the station that night, right then, and then the next day, like a little kid. He got so excited thinking about what he might find, I had to say no about ten times, because one thing I knew was that we had to be there, in Behala, for the big search – especially if the policemen who talked to us were there.

I had to get a hold of his hair and I said, 'How is it going to look when everyone is there to earn money, and the boy they know found something – maybe a shoe, or maybe something else – doesn't show?'

Raphael is my best friend but he's like a kid, always laughing, playing, thinking everything's fun, thinking it's a game – so I said they have to see us working and looking, and that way maybe they leave us alone: and so we waited.

Next morning, like I said, the whole of Behala turns out, early and ready, before dawn. Like Raphael said, we get money for what we can sell, hand to mouth, so getting paid for the day is like a dream, and there were way too many pickers – I guess people had told people, and there were crowds of us, all piling in. Then the police arrived early also, and even as the sun came up, everyone was way up on the trash – men, women and every damn kid, even the tiny ones – earning their precious hundred, some without even hooks, just using hands – in fact, there were so many of us, it was dangerous, and you could feel the trash sliding about, and there was no room to throw the stuff you'd sorted.

I was hooking stuff up, scratching other people almost, and it was more and more dangerous, so after one hour all us kids were ordered off, and just the men stayed on, and the trash was being gone through again – right by where we'd been the previous day. The managers were there, talking to the police, shouting up to the men – and it was all being picked over and over, again and again. But nothing was coming up.

All the while, more cars – police car, then another police car, then a police truck, motorbikes, more police cars, and then big cars like government cars – and men in suits as well as police, getting out and their nice shoes getting wet and filthy. And it's still not seven o'clock and you can't move for the cars and people, like it's a festival.

No belts were working, as they turned them all off.

Things get worse.

Soon we can see the line of trucks coming in is stretching right back through the gates and down the road, waiting to unload: after just one hour I'd counted twenty-six. The drivers didn't even care at first – they squatted in the shade, and some boys went off to get them tea and cigarettes. There were kids jumping into the trucks then, and picking there, on the roadside, but me and Raphael stayed down, listening around for more 'information', me wondering all the time where this was going to end – knowing, because I knew, that people were going to be angry soon, and it would be these police losing patience first. When the police get mean, you don't want to be around. On the other hand, I did not want Raphael hiding and drawing attention that way, so that was why I kept him right in the middle of it.

One man had a box with a great wad of notes in it, and he'd shown it around to prove we'd all be paid. I overheard another one talking, and I worked out what was happening – they were using their brains. Somehow they knew the bag had been lost in this place called McKinley – which is a rich area – so it wasn't hard to trace the trucks that look after that neighbourhood. Now, the McKinley trucks had made one visit yesterday, which is how we found what we found – and more were coming in again today. So, for today's trucks, all the police had to do was get them to drop the loads on a clear patch of ground, and we could pick over it easy, in an hour.

Sure enough, just before noon they brought up the three special McKinley trucks and they dropped their loads, and they kept us all back, so we were all just looking at it. I said to Raphael then, turning him round so no one saw: 'Are you still sure, friend?'

He was looking scared because I think he was just beginning to realize how big this must be.

He said, very soft, 'I'm more sure than ever, Gardo,' so I stayed close.

We tried to look just happy and excited then, because the last thing I wanted was for anyone to think we were suspicious or scared or worried or hiding something – but I was frightened too, and I grabbed Raphael and made sure we joined in the pushing and shoving, like we hadn't a care in the world. When we saw Rat, we waved: he was squatting close by, smoking, and he would look over at me sometimes, but nobody looked at him, because Rat is grey as trash, and he has only the clothes he wears, which are so filthy he can move around and no one sees him.

After a while the police gathered all us kids together and got us working – they'd got extra hooks from somewhere, and as we were on level ground it wasn't a hard job: we just ripped and ripped, and spread it all out.

There were about a hundred of us.

The people in McKinley have toilets, so there wasn't any stupp – McKinley trash is good-quality trash: food, newspaper, a lot of plastic and glass, but the police wouldn't let us take anything, because as far as they were concerned, we were looking for just one thing.

Then someone found a handbag, and there was real excitement, lots of shouting: it was blue, and old, with one stringy little handle, so it was thrown back, everyone very disappointed, and the police just watched us work, looking grim and their patience running out.

By mid-afternoon, I guess, we'd finished, and I don't think a pile of rubbish had ever got a better looking at: the men on the trash piles had finished as well, and everyone was ordered down. Of course, we all would have worked for the rest of the day, and the rest of the week – we were hoping to string it out and get five hundred out of it – but the police were smart, and could see that even in a mountain of rubbish, you can pick through what's up top pretty fast, and you can see what's new and what isn't.

I saw the boxer policeman was back – the big guy who'd made the speech yesterday – and he was talking it all over with the site managers and two men in suits by one of the big black cars. There was a lot of arguing going on, a lot of calls being made, and I could see the managers weren't happy – I think because the line of loaded trucks was getting longer and longer, and the drivers were finally getting itchy, drinking tea all day and not knowing when they were going home. And you could see what the problem was: if the police allowed these trucks to unload new, fresh trash, the precious bag was going to be buried even further down, if it was there. But on the other hand, this was the city dumpsite, and how long can

34

you close down a dump when all these millions of people are sending stuff to it? How long before the city stops?

But what must have been burning them up was that no one could be sure the bag had ever got here. After all, kids go through the trash straight out of the bins, in McKinley same as everywhere. Sometimes you see them in the street, sorting on the pavements. Also, like I said, kids get up inside the carts before they've even reached the dump – so they could not know the bag had even got to the dumpsite. It was strange to think there were just three boys in the world who knew exactly where it was.

* * *

We all sat around.

Money got paid out at last, and everyone was one hundred pesos richer. It was getting dark, the sky red all over, and the police finally gave up and started leaving, me and Raphael smiling. Then all the belts started with a sound that splits your ears, and the trucks started crawling through again, and they brought out more lights and worked on and on, right through until the morning.

In our little neighbourhood there were more cooking fires than usual, and a few cases of beer. There was music and singing, and everyone was happy – most of all Raphael, who thinks the job is done and he's been so smart.

But inside Raphael's house, right by me – because I

was staying close now – after the food, his auntie says to both of us: 'Are we safe?'

I knew she wasn't, and I also knew she'd brought it on herself. Opening her mouth had not been smart – in fact, I hate to say it, but we talked about it since: if she had kept her mouth shut, things would have been so much easier. 'Are we safe?' she said again.

I said, 'We are completely safe. Don't worry,' which was a lie.

'I was spoken to,' she said to me. 'They wanted to know why I said he found something. A policeman asked me about it again, and I shouldn't have spoken, but I did. Now they're wondering about both of you. They got both your names.'

'Yes, but we told them,' said Raphael, doing his smile and pushing back his hair, 'it was just a shoe, and they know nothing.'

She was quiet, but only for a moment.

'I saw you go out last night,' she said, very soft like you could hardly hear, so we were huddling close. 'I don't want to know where, I don't want to know why, but I just want to know we're safe. There's nothing in the house, is there?'

We both said: 'No.'

'You promise me that? Because they will take these houses apart—'

'I promise,' said Raphael, so light and bright. All I

could think about was the lies, stacking up now, and how I hoped it was worth it. The bag was safe, down with Rat – I wanted to get away and check it.

Raphael's auntie kept at him, though: 'They're talking about searching here,' she said. 'That's what people say. Ours will be the first, you can bet on that. If they take it apart again—'

Raphael took her hand then: 'There's nothing in the house,' he said.

'Ten thousand is a lot of money!' she said, and her voice rose up. 'Have you thought what we could do with that?'

I interrupted then. 'You think they'd give it?' I said. 'You really think they'd give it?'

'I think they would!' she said.

Raphael shook her hand gently. 'Ma,' he said. 'Ma. If someone here – one of us – if one of us got all that money, you think we'd be allowed to keep it for long?'

She reached out to me then, and took hold of my arm, so we were all three linked together. 'You're smart,' she said to me. 'Gardo, you're smarter than this boy, and I know you can run fast and get clear – and maybe I shouldn't have spoken, and I'm sorry I did. But I'm too old to move again, and the two little ones . . .'

Her eyes were all full of tears, glittering wet – and I got scared because she was scared, and I know Raphael was most scared of all, though he won't ever say so.

'I don't want us getting caught up with the police,' she said, gripping us hard. 'Everyone knows what things they do.'

I couldn't meet her eye.

For one thing, I was mad she'd spoken up – it was still the dumbest thing she could have done. For another, I had a feeling things were going to get bad. Sure, I wanted to be smart, like she said I was, and I knew I had to lead this, because Raphael needs to be led. I needed to keep a hold of him.

I was planning it fast, and that's why I said nothing.

We just had to get to the railway station – that's what I thought. We had to find out what was in the locker, and do it fast. Then, maybe, in a few days' time, we could give up the wallet with the key inside it and get everyone off our backs.

If that was too suspicious, I could get Rat to give it up – nobody would suspect him, because he worked alone, he didn't talk to people. So I thought, *Let Rat be the little hero and bring them what they wanted in a few days' time.*

But if even that was too dangerous, I was thinking – then we could just throw the wallet and key up into the trash, and wait till somebody – anybody – found it, if they ever did.

There was nothing in the house, that was true – and nobody could prove anything, and we were *not* in danger, and we could still make money – that is what I told myself, and Raphael was thinking just the same kind of thing, and we talked it through all night, thinking we were being smart and so not knowing what we were getting into. Not dealing with the fact that if the police think you've got something, they won't stop till they've got it from you.

6

Raphael again.

The next day Gardo let us go to the station. I told him me and Rat would go alone if he didn't.

He said, what if we were being watched? I couldn't see how they could watch us with us not seeing them, and I said we'd be moving so fast they'd never know.

He said, what if they come back to the dumpsite, looking for us? I said, what if they don't?

He said, what if they've got the station staked out? And I said, what if we just do nothing for ever and forget the whole thing? Is that what he wanted? He kind of snarled at me then, but I'd got my way.

So, early morning we went down to the tracks. The trains cut through the south side of Behala, very close to the docks. If you want to get to Central, you can pick one up ten minutes from my house.

People have built their homes right up to the line, because the ground is flat and clear. Every now and again the homes get torn down and the people get shipped out. Over time, they come back, and the game starts again. It's not as dangerous as you might think, because the trains are only four a day just there, and they go slow. They're long and heavy, and you can hear them coming a mile away. The only person I ever heard of getting run over by a train was a woman about two years ago, and she did it on purpose, walking up as the train came and laying her head right on the rail.

Gardo, me and Rat waited for the six o'clock. It came by pretty much on time, and we ran alongside the last coach. It's a passenger train, and it goes for nine hours, way down to a town called Diamond Harbour. It starts at the docks, but not many people get on there. Then it goes to Central, where it gets so full you can't breathe. We swung up and in through the windows – there's no glass and no bars – and the only people were an old couple at one end, so we spread ourselves over the benches, and looked out and waved like we were on holiday.

'What if they're watching?' said Gardo again. When he gets something on his mind, you can't ever get it off again.

'How can they be?' said Rat.

'They'd be looking for people doing anything suspicious. How many times have we been on a train, Raphael?'

'I don't know, not often—'

'They're police, yes? They're gonna be looking out to see what we're doing. What if they know there was a locker key – they just don't know the number?'

'No, listen,' I said. 'That's crazy. If they know the bag

41

had a locker key, they'd have broken into every locker in the station. They cannot know what's in the bag.'

'Maybe they're at the station now, opening every locker. Waiting for us.'

'If they are, we just walk away. We're just three boys out roaming.'

Rat said nothing. He just looked from me to Gardo and back again, and when I caught his eye, he smiled and we both laughed.

Gardo told us to shut up. 'Twenty thousand now,' he said. 'That's the prize money they're offering, I heard – they just doubled it.'

'You know they won't pay it.'

'What I'm saying is, whatever they're looking for is getting more important. If this José Angelico killed someone – what if he killed an important man – a politician, maybe: someone rich – and we've got the clues to catch the guy? What are we going to do then? We end up stopping the police catching a killer—'

I said, 'Gardo, why don't we just see what's in the locker?' And I smiled right at him and lay back on the bench. 'We decide what to do then, OK?' I told him to rest his brain.

'I do the locker,' said Rat.

We both looked at him, and Gardo asked him what he meant.

'I best do the locker,' he said. 'OK? I best square it with

the station boys too – say we're just doing an errand for someone, give them something. Also, in case anyone's looking . . . I know where it is. I'll go in fast, grab what's there – meet you back by the tracks. Anyone sees me, I just run. Three of us run, they'll get one of us. If it's me, I'll lose them. OK?'

'How much to the station boys?' I said. 'They going to want how much?'

'I don't know. I'll try twenty and make it look like a small thing. Give me a hundred, though.'

I gave Rat the notes, and he was twitching a little, getting scared. Gardo was shaking his head, thinking deep. He said: 'It's a good idea, Rat. I can see where you're coming from. But I say stick together. We ought to stay together in this.' He looked at me and said, 'You better stay close to me!'

Minutes later, the train was slowing for the station, and we stood out on the sides. I could see the platform coming up, so I jumped and ended up rolling on the grass. Gardo nearly fell on me, but Rat stayed on his feet. I hadn't seen before just how quick Rat could be, and he was so thin it was like he was just straws and paper, like he could blow off in the wind like a little kite. He didn't even look round, he just skipped along, and we hurried after him. We ran up onto the platforms, and a couple of kids looked at us with a kind of mean-eyed suspicion, like this was their territory – which it was.

They followed us up, at a distance.

We jumped early because you don't ever want to be seen getting off the train. If guards or even porters see you, you can get a real thrashing. The station boys are different. As long as they don't steal or get in the way, nobody cares too much. They keep the station clean, and go through a train in about two minutes. If they beg or sell, they know to do it off at the sides – that's why people let them alone.

So now we were all making our way up the platform, just a straggling bunch of three barefoot boys; we might have been invisible. I knew the dangerous bit was going to be the locker, because that was something you did not usually see. Boys like us opening luggage lockers? It wouldn't have to be police. It would be anyone who noticed. They'd assume right away that we were thieving, and thieving boys get no mercy from anyone.

Just off the platform we were met by more station boys and these ones were bigger. We got kind of herded over to the side and I could feel Gardo getting ready, feeling for his hook, which he always carries somewhere. Rat did the talking though, since he used to live there and knew some of them, and I saw him pass over the twenty – then another fifty, then a twenty. Everyone shook hands, and they let us go. I guess Rat had paid for them not to follow us, because we went on alone to the main station square.

'They give us five minutes,' he said.

It's a giant station, and that time in the morning it's just getting crazy – a good time for us, but scary as hell. You got porters, you got travelling families, you got trucks delivering stuff, horns blasting, train whistles, loud speakers. Everyone's cutting in and out of everyone else, and the noise is so loud you have to shout. Rat kept moving fast, and I was beginning to get frightened again. I hadn't liked the look of the station boys, but now – everywhere I looked I could see mean-looking railway guards – and we were getting stared at. I had to keep saying to myself, 'We're not breaking the law' – but it felt like we were, and everyone knows stories about what happens to kids if they get caught breaking the law. I don't mean what I said about just riding in a train and being thrashed. We've got prisons in this city, and the prisons take kids quicker than they take men. You also hear stories of boys not even making it to prison, but I don't know how much truth there is in any of it – everyone's out to scare you with a story. I was told once about runaways, and it made me sick. How if a new kid shows up with nowhere to go, and the police get him – they wait till night, break his legs and put him on the tracks. They're stories, and they may not be true, but I couldn't stop thinking of them as I walked across that station, feeling small – nearly losing Rat, but Gardo by my side, up close. Both of us just waiting to be caught.

Rat kept going. Somehow he'd shaken off that twitch

he gets, and was walking fast, looking happy as a kid. He stayed a little bit ahead of us. He had something in his hand, and I saw it was the key, so I guessed we must be near. We went under a bridge into some kind of hall with a low ceiling and lines of tube-lights. We kept walking, like we knew where we were going, and there they were: two long aisles of grey metal lockers – lines and lines of doors.

We kept on walking.

Some doors were big enough to take suitcases, and some, up above, were small enough for just a handbag. There were no police, no guards – no station boys – and Rat knew exactly where he was going, and he hung back for a moment so we drew level, and he said, 'You keep moving, OK? Walk.'

There were two women opening one locker, and we went straight past them. They were far too busy with whatever it was they were putting in to notice us. A tall man at the far end was locking a door, and his back was to us. I could see the numbers: 110, 109, 108 – none of them were smashed, everything was neat and quite new, and there were still no police. Then, suddenly, Rat had turned and he had the key in the lock. We walked straight past him, and we heard the sound of metal. Nobody shouted, nobody even noticed. I was ten paces on when I heard the sound of a door closing, and then Rat was next to us again, and I could see he had something under his arm.

'Don't run,' he said. 'Slow down, OK?'

We did as he said but my heart was pounding. Gardo was smart enough to stop and play with a drinks machine, checking the slot for money. I was thinking, *Look like nothing's wrong!* – three station kids making their way. Rat had the package under his shirt now. We went out onto platform four, and right along to the end, weaving through the people. We did start to run then, out of relief. We got down on the tracks, and we started to run fast. Five minutes later, we got among bushes and bramble, and there was a small pile of concrete sleepers to sit on, and we were out of breath.

Rat was grinning and laughing, and I was as well. He held the package in both hands, and offered it up like a present. It was a brown envelope, sealed up with tape, and it took me some time to get it open.

Inside was a letter, with a stamp in the corner, waiting to be posted.

There was writing in a thick pen: *If found, please deliver.* Then the address: *Gabriel Olondriz* was the name. Underneath that: *Prisoner 746229, Cell Block 34K, South Wing, Colva Prison.*

I felt myself go cold again, but I grinned up at Gardo and he looked hard, right at me.

I opened the letter and read it out loud. One page, and a little slip stuck to it, with just a line of numbers, making no sense. Then again, the letter made no sense: we understood none of it. All we were sure of was that we were in something deep, getting deeper.

940.4.18.13.14./5.3.6.4./9.1.12.10.3.3./12.9.2.3.25.32./
6.1.6.2.1.11./3.3.3.2.1.6.15.5.1.6/5.11.1.6./2.4.5.2.5.4./3.1.4.1.4.1
.13.28/2.16.4.7.7.1./5.9.11.2.5.6./2.7.6.2.7.2.21.7.7.3.7.5.1.2.1.1.
7.5./16.3.7.9.12.6.4.3.5.1./1.4.11.3./2.6.3.1.1.2.1.9.1.4.

PART TWO

1

My name is Father Juilliard, and I am the one pulling these accounts together – all names changed, for obvious reasons. You will understand the importance of this at the end: but it's a story that had to be told. The next set of events is best left to me, and to one of my former staff.

I will just tell you that I have been running the Pascal Aguila Mission School on the Behala dumpsite for seven years. It was going to be a one-year job: my task was to set it back on its feet after some financial mismanagement. It was to be my final posting – I'm sixty-three. But I fell in love with the place, and have been here ever since. Unfortunately I am being retired this year – partly because of this story. The school has already appointed its new head, and my final official task is the handover.

I hope to stay in the country, but I'm not sure I can.

I should say, by the way, that our school does need new energy, as we've been getting smaller rather than larger. It's hard to keep the children attending class: we have to bribe them with food. Our income's going down, and the food resources are never regular. It's also so hot, and around the dry season it gets stifling. The school is made of large metal boxes – the iron containers you see on ships and trucks. Ten were donated to start the Mission. They were bolted together, and windows and doors were hacked out – there it was, an instant metal school. Six more crates were bought, and they made the upstairs. Two form a chapel. Three have been knocked together for a babies' room, with a little play area in one corner. Half of one is a rest area, and the other half is my office.

I only knew Raphael and Gardo by sight, as they rarely came to classes. Few children do after the age of ten. Their families want them picking trash, and it's hard to argue that education's ever going to be helpful – so we lose them. Little Jun – the boy they call 'Rat' – I knew better. He would visit me in my office, sneaking up when the other children had gone, climbing the outside like a monkey. I'd let him in through a window, I'd give him the ointments and plasters he needed, and – if he wanted one – I'd let him take a bath. I would have to give him food too, because he was evidently starving. We had a rule that food was only provided at lunch time and for half an hour after classes. I broke that rule for Jun, and a handful of others like him, because I have always said that you have to break the rules. I set rules up; then I break them. Sister Olivia broke the rules as well, as you shall hear.

Don't put your feet on the chairs, don't take more food than food for you – don't take food out to your family. Stay in line, say the prayer quietly, wear a shirt when you're indoors, wash your feet before chapel – I have to laugh myself, but rules are what we live by even though we all know they're sometimes foolish. One rule that I like a lot, though, is an unusual one: *on the stairs up to chapel, nobody must speak.*

Why can't you speak on the chapel stairs? Let me tell you – somewhere it is relevant.

The steps and the chapel are dedicated to the man whose name we bear – Pascal Aguila – one of the country's lesser-known freedom fighters. The Aguila family donates a large sum of money every year, and they bought those last six containers for our upstairs. They ask that we honour Pascal's memory – which is a pleasure as well as a duty. He was a man who fought corruption and was shot to death for his pains, so we honour him several times a day, just by being quiet on the stairs. I find that the children never need reminding. Just now and then, if there's a boy or girl who's new, they might be chattering; then you hear a great gust of 'Shhhhh', like a breeze, and everyone is silent. We tell them about Pascal, of course, and his picture hangs over the altar. He was a man determined to build things and make life better. He spoke a dozen languages, yet he was from a poor family. He became a lawyer, but he continued to live in a poor quarter of the city. He took on impossible cases, and won them. When squatters had their houses bulldozed, Pascal Aguila forced the government to find them land. When a building project hired a thousand men and failed to supply them with boots, gloves or hats, Pascal Aguila sued, and forced a change in the law that made the construction industry a whole lot safer. When cholera hit the swamps, just up from the docks, Pascal Aguila forced the local hospital – a private concern, for the paying rich – to set up a special unit for the poor. His final act – the one that killed him – was to expose three senators who'd been siphoning off public taxes and stowing them off-shore. They all resigned, and the prosecution rumbles on. Pascal Aguila was shot to pieces in a taxi, on his way to testify. Twenty-six bullets – the same calibre as a policeman's gun, and his murderers were never found.

I sometimes sit on the stairs, under the plaque we had made, and I think about this brave man. It is by such small things – small as a silent staircase – that the dead live on and help us. In this country, the dead are very important.

You want to know how I was part of Raphael's tale, of course, and what I did. I was on the edge, only. Sister Olivia, our temporary house-mother, was more crucial, and perhaps more foolish – but I got involved because of the school computer, which was donated by the RCBC bank. We score these little successes! We get our foot in the door. You won't think me uncharitable, I hope, when I confess that the computer was old and out of date, and if they hadn't given it to us, it would have ended on one of the trash heaps. Who cares? They gave with a good heart, I think, and we have had much use out of it. It connects to the Internet, and the children play games on it when I let them.

It was a Thursday afternoon when Jun came by, with the two boys I hardly knew.

'Sir po,' he said. 'Sir po?'

He's got a high-pitched, musical little voice, and I recognized it instantly.

I turned and smiled, and he was leaning on my office door. He's thin as a match, and the colour of ash. He has a smile that makes me smile too, and I'm always pleased to see him. 'We are looking for something, po.' 'Po', by the way, is the word of respect people use here for their elders. 'Can we use the computer, sir po?'

I told him it was late. Then I looked beyond him, and saw he had two friends with him – slight, skinny boys. One looked shy and the other looked watchful – you could see at once who the leader was. His head was shaved and his eyes didn't blink. He had long arms and, even with the poor diet he had, the poise – the grace – of an athlete. The other one had long hair over his face, and another enchanting smile.

'Po, sir po. This is Gardo.' He pointed at the boy with the shaved head. 'This is Raphael – d'you know them?'

I told him I didn't but was pleased to – and we all shook hands.

'They're taking part in a quiz,' said Jun. 'It's a newspaper thing, sir. They have to research, sir. They said they don't come to school here so why would you help them, so I said I'd come. They can give money for the computer time, OK? I said maybe you would, po.'

I told them to come in, and they came over to my desk. Shorts and T-shirts, bare feet black right up to their knees – their smell filled the room. The one called Raphael looked at me, pushing his hair back, too shy to make eye contact. He held a twenty-peso note in both his hands, for computer time. Gardo stayed behind him, and I could feel him staring right at me, as if he might have to fight.

'I'm afraid the connection's slow today,' I said.

I put a second chair by the computer, and waved away the boy's money. They slid onto the chairs, and Raphael got straight down to work. Children always know how to use computers – it never fails to amaze me. Children who'd never stepped inside a classroom could work a keyboard faster than me. It was the games shops where they learned, of course. For ten pesos you could get fifteen minutes of shooting and chasing.

I saw him go straight to a search engine, and the bald boy opened a piece of paper. Raphael tapped in a name, and we all watched as the computer thought long and hard.

I said: 'What have you eaten today, Jun?'

He smiled up at me and held my arm. 'Nothing!' he said proudly.

I went down to the kitchen and made some sandwiches. I got three glasses too, and filled them with lemonade. By the time I got back, the boys were chattering in low, excited voices, scrolling down the screen and pointing. They'd called up a local news site, and were reading carefully.

'What's the question?' I said. They looked blank, so I said, 'For your quiz? What question are you answering?'

Raphael said, 'It's about history, sir.' Then he was talking in his own language, which I am ashamed to say I hardly speak, despite the length of time I've been out here. The second boy, Gardo, was shaking his head. Whatever they were looking at seemed to be a serious business.

Jun, meanwhile, took a sandwich in a hand that was so dirty it made me wince. The boy bites his nails right down to the quick, and his fingers remind me of skeletons. He promises and promises to come to class, but he so rarely does – he must have the strangest mix of ideas from the ones he's attended! It's become a joke between us. I always say, 'So – you'll be in school tomorrow?' He assures me that he will, and I know he won't. I will never forget the sight of him the first time he took a shower here. He had a towel wrapped round himself, and was dancing with the cold and the excitement of the spurting water – and maybe the amazement of seeing his own flesh looking clean. I gave him one of our school uniforms, but I never saw him wear it.

Sister Olivia fell in love with him too, and asked me about adoption. A twenty-two-year-old girl from England, wanting to adopt! I told her not to think of it. The machinery for adoption out here is slow, for one thing. In six years I've known one successful case for a foreigner. No government is going to give away its children, I understand that – and yet you look around at the thousands who cannot be taken care of and it breaks your heart. You look at the mountains of garbage, and the children on them, like so much more garbage, and it's easy to think what you do in a school like this is of absolutely no consequence or good to anyone. More and more children. When I walk around the shanties, I see the babies, and I am always asked to hold them. And while we're smiling and laughing, I am thinking, in the back of my mind: *This tiny child – as soon as it can crawl, it will be crawling through trash.*

The boys finished on the computer soon after I came back with the tray, and they turned and had a sandwich, and drank their lemonade. They were polite, as the children here always are, but they wanted to go.

I said, 'So. School tomorrow? All three of you?'

Jun laughed. 'Definitely!'

Raphael said, 'I want to come, po. But I'm working.'

He pushed his hair back and smiled his dazzling smile.

I reminded him that he could work and also do a morning class. I reminded him that the school was set up for exactly that purpose: to let the children work while providing education. If they attend five days, they get two kilos of rice and a few bits and pieces extra, depending on what's been donated – that is the incentive. Raphael looked at me, and I wondered if he was thinking that obvious thought: *And what use is an education to me?*

He said, 'I will come, po.'

Then Jun took the plate and glasses into my kitchen. He insisted on washing them, and setting them in the drying rack. Then he gave me a hug and I slipped him fifty pesos.

The other boys were waiting for him outside, and they ran away together – I never saw them again. It was a few weeks later that I discovered they'd been lying. There had been no quiz, of course. They were finding out everything they could about Mr José Angelico, the man whose ID they'd found. They'd also been researching Gabriel Olondriz, who at that time was serving his twenty-third year in the city's biggest prison.

Rat had been up to something too, which he will reveal in due course. They had all got what they wanted, and had deceived me beautifully.

2

This is Raphael again, and now it gets serious.

The police came that night, just like Gardo said they would, and searched our house. I was arrested.

Four van-loads came, and everyone in the block was ordered out. They had flashlights and batons, and they moved through fast while more and more people gathered, up from the other neighbourhoods. The police said nothing to anyone. They showed some bit of paper to Thomas – our senior man – and they didn't wait for him to say anything. Then it took them less than an hour, and we all stood listening as they shouted to each other and threw things. Some of the little kids were crying, but most people were calm, just watching.

What could anyone do?

Then they got back in the vans, having found nothing.

I had not thought they would take me, because nobody had said anything to me. I saw the young policeman again, and I saw him nod in my direction, and I realized they were talking about me. It still came as a surprise – I don't know why – when two police came over and took hold of my arms.

This is going to be very difficult to write about, the next part, but it's only me that can.

I did not know what to do. I did not make a sound, and I did not move – I was too scared to breathe and I didn't know which man to look up at. Gardo was right with me at once, and he was talking fast, saying, 'What are you doing? What's he done?' over and over, touching me. My auntie started to scream, and then she fell down on the ground. Immediately there was a great commotion, and I saw how important it was that I was not taken. People were shouting; some were pleading with the policemen, and getting between me and the car. One of the vans had stopped, and some police were coming back, but before I could take in any more, I was walked to the car that had its door open, my arms held hard. Gardo got his arm round me, but someone pushed him off, and I heard him shouting over the top of everyone else, but one of his uncles had hold of him. I got to the car and I tried to back off, but I was dragged and pushed. I was between two big men, and whatever I said, nobody heard me – I twisted, but I was just picked up, and I was in the back seat. Doors slammed, and I saw Gardo again. He was screaming at me, trying to get to me, and a policeman grabbed him by the neck and threw him off. Then the car was moving and I was crying. I saw faces through the window, staring at me, shouting at me, but I couldn't see anyone I knew, and Gardo was gone.

I was so frightened I felt sick and I couldn't stop crying.

We were bumping and rocking because the road is so rutted and the driver was going as fast as he could. There was still a crowd around me, and someone was banging on the roof – and then we were through the gates, and on the road. They put their siren on, and we whipped through. Red lights didn't matter, the traffic police waved us on. For some reason it didn't feel quite so bad when we were going past stores, and the roads were full of people, and everything was lit up. But when we turned off into smaller roads, there were no people, and soon there were no lights.

I have never felt so lost and lonely, and I still could not stop crying. I said, 'Where are we going?'

One man said, 'Where do you think we're going?'

I said, 'I haven't done anything, sir.'

The man said, 'Keep still, boy – we know that.'

'I haven't done anything, sir,' I said again. I kept saying it through my sobs.

I tried to keep still, like the man had told me to, but I couldn't. I was rocking backwards and forwards. All you can think about is how alone you are, and how anything can happen now. A little while ago, things had felt safe and ordinary – my auntie, Gardo, the cousins, the fire – and people, all around me. Now! It is like falling through a trapdoor. In a second, every single thing had changed, and you are falling – your friends cannot get to you, nobody knows where you are, and you think, *So when do I stop falling?* You think, *What plan do they have for me that I can do nothing about?*

Rat had the envelope. Rat had the ID. I would not give either of them up because we knew more now. We knew about José Angelico, and there was a fight beginning.

The streets and buildings were all grey-cement coloured, and we drove left, right, up, down, and came round fast into a car park, up close to a heavy-looking gate. A policeman with a dog opened it, and we drove through, and down a ramp. To be going down, underground, was more frightening still, and I started to cry harder. I called for my auntie as well, and that is when – I will be honest – I wet myself.

We stopped in bright lights, and I was taken out of the car. I could hardly move by myself, and a policeman had to pull me – not because I was resisting, but because I was so frightened my legs wouldn't work. He spoke quite softly and put his arm round me, half carrying me. We went down some steps and through metal doors. We came to a corridor, and there were cells on either side of it, all with numbers. A policeman opened one of the doors, and I was put inside. The door closed and I stood there, not knowing what to do, feeling so sick I thought I would fall over and die. Seconds later, the door opened again with lots of noise, and a policeman came in and told me to sit down.

I sat on the floor, and I was sick. I hadn't eaten much, but up it came and went all over my knees, and I started crying again, and I had never before heard the sounds that I was making – I had never cried like I was crying then.

The policeman sat on the bench, and he didn't close the door this time. I think he realized that I was too frightened to be left alone and that somebody should be with me. The policeman gave me a little towel, and I tried to clean myself, but my hands would not work.

Time passed.

There was nothing in the cell but the bench, which was concrete. The policeman said a few things to me, just casual questions about who I was. I found that I couldn't speak, much as I tried to. After a while, a man in a light grey suit came in and looked at me. He asked me my name. I managed to say it, but my voice wasn't my voice.

'Six,' he said. 'We'll use six.'

He went out, and two policemen came and lifted me to my feet. They had to almost carry me. I was taken back along the corridor, and this time up some steps instead of down. We climbed high and then passed some offices, with policemen working in them. Nobody looked up. We turned some corners, and I remember a sign board with pictures of a beach, and there was a list of names. I saw a clock, and it said two-twenty. Then we went into a room with a number six chalked on the door, and there was a metal table with the man in the suit sitting at it, having got there ahead of us. Behind him, standing, was the important police officer who had first come to Behala – the rough guy with the smashed nose. Behind him was a window, and next to him was a third man in shirt sleeves, bald and sweaty and angry and tired-looking.

I was put in a chair.

'Raphael,' said the tired man. 'Raphael Fernández? You know where you are?'

I shook my head.

'You're in Ermita Police Station. You know why you're here?'

I shook my head again, and tried to speak. Nothing came out.

'We need the bag you found,' said the policeman.

There was silence then, and my throat was so dry I had no idea what my voice would sound like if I managed to say something. But I tried and tried, and the words came from somewhere. 'I didn't find a bag, sir,' I said. Still I didn't recognize this voice that was coming out of me.

'This isn't going to end, Raphael, until you give us the bag.'

'I didn't find a bag, sir,' I said. I had to make myself a child – just a terrified, foolish child. 'I promise, sir. I swear.'

A cup of water was put next to me, and when I tried to pick it up, I spilled it. I started to cry again, and I wanted to go to the toilet. The tired man waited while someone mopped up the water.

'All you have to do,' he said, 'is take us back to your house. Give us the bag – wherever you put it. We give you money, like we said we would. Everyone's happy.'

I managed to look at him.

'I swear to God, sir. I swear on my mother's soul: I did not find a bag. I found money. I found eleven hundred pesos, and that's all—'

'You found money.'

'Yes, sir.'

'So you *did* lie? You *did* find something?'

'Yes, sir, I did.'

'Where did you find it? When?'

'By belt number four. Thursday afternoon.' I was lying. I didn't want them to know where I'd been. The problem is, your own lies can trap you. The man in the grey suit was writing things down.

'Who were you with? Who saw you?'

'Nobody, sir. I was—'

'That's a lie,' said the policeman, and he came at me from the side. I don't know where he hit me or what with, but I was knocked to the floor. My chair turned over and the side of my face was split. I fell badly, and my wrist was bent under me, and I saw him standing over me and I thought he was going to start kicking. I screamed, 'No! No! No!' over and over again, and tried to get under the table. The policeman didn't kick me. He reached down, grabbed me, and he and the man in the suit lifted me up by the hair and an arm, and I was put back in the chair. Someone had me by the hair still.

'I was with Gardo,' I shouted. There was blood in my mouth. 'Just my friend! But I didn't give him money! He didn't see me find it. I'm sorry, I'm sorry! I was with Gardo, and I found some money – I did not . . .' I started to sob. 'I did not find a bag!'

'And the shoe?' said the policeman behind me. He was the one holding my hair. 'What about the shoe?'

'I didn't find a shoe, I was lying!' I cried. I tried to wipe my face, but it was all blood and snot, and I was slapped again, hard, so that lights were flashing. 'I found the money!' I shouted. 'I didn't want to . . .' I was panting for breath, and I started to sob. The policeman was leaning over me, one big hand on the table, one hand twisting my hair.

'What was the money in?' said the suit man. 'Leave him alone.'

'It was wrapped up in paper,' I said. 'I think it was a bill.'

'Eleven hundred pesos, wrapped in a bill?'

'It was an electricity bill, sir. I think. It was orange, and I think they're the electrical bills.' I was thinking so fast, just fighting for my life.

'You can read, can you?' said the man in the suit. 'This piece of shit can read?'

'Yes, sir, I can read!'

'How's that? Huh?' He stood opposite me, leaned in and lifted my face. I could smell his cigarettes and his sweat. 'Who taught trash like you to read? What's your name?'

'Raphael, sir—'

'Who taught you to read?'

'Gardo, and my auntie.'

'What kind of bill? What address?'

'I didn't see, I didn't look.'

'How much money?'

'Eleven hundred.'

'Exactly eleven hundred? How many notes?'

'One five, six ones.'

'Where are they now?'

'I gave them to my auntie. I kept one for myself.'

'What about the bag?'

'No bag, sir.'

'I'm going to kill you, you liar!' He lunged at me, and I was falling backwards, but the policeman lifted me and the suit man had my throat. I was up against the wall, and that is when I lost control and simply . . . all down my legs, I lost control – I was so frightened – and I was stinking, and I was shouting, 'I didn't find a bag, sir!'

'Get him out – get rid of him!'

I was lifted up and they were carrying me to the window. The man in the suit was opening it, I was held by the policeman by my ankle and my arm, and I was going towards it sideways – it was coming at me, this big open window. I remember warm air. I remember suddenly I was out, and the hand holding my arm let go, and I was upside down, held by just one ankle – I could see the filthy wall: it was like a pit – and a long way down below me I could see a stone floor with what looked like trash cans. I was screaming so much now, and when I looked up they were all looking down at me.

'Where's the bag?' shouted one of them. 'Did you find it?'

All I could shout was no. Gardo has asked me – Rat too – did I come close to giving in? And the truth is, no, I did not. It sounds crazy, but there was a part of me sure I'd never found it, and some other part of me begging me not to give it up – maybe for José Angelico, because we knew more about him now. The hand on my ankle was tight, and I knew any second it could let me go and I would fall. I would fall on my head and be broken. The man was shaking me, and everything was spinning, and there was blood, sweat, my own mess, and the walls turning, but I would not say anything other than no, and they would believe me or it would just be over.

I was suddenly dragged up.

They hauled me in over the edge so all my chest was cut, but I hardly knew it at the time. I was stood up and slapped again, and then they all waited.

I fell on my knees, and they let me.

I managed to take hold of somebody's leg, and held it – I put my head on my hands. I was down there, kneeling, and I said, 'I swear on my mother's soul I did not find a bag. I am telling the truth, sir – please don't kill me. I cannot help you, I am speaking the truth.'

Where did I find the strength? I know that it was José Angelico's strength.

'I am sorry,' I said, and I was fighting for my life, and knew it. 'I should have told you I found money, but I should have given it to my friend also, and I didn't so I lied to you. Please don't kill me, please.'

'What belt were you under?' said the policeman.

'Four, sir, honestly – I promise.'

'Where's the bill the money was wrapped in?'

'I put it in the paper sack. I put the money in my pocket.'

'Raphael, listen to me.'

This was the man in the suit, I think. He knelt down next to me, but my head was throbbing so badly I cannot really remember.

'You're the breadwinner, aren't you, for your stinking little family?'

I nodded, but I didn't look up. 'Yes, sir.'

'If anything happened to you, your family would have big, big problems. What would your auntie do?'

'I don't know, sir.'

'Two little cousins – what would happen to them? Can you hear me?'

'Yes – I don't know, sir. I didn't find a bag, sir, please believe me.'

'We can drop you out of that window. Or we can take you out the back. We can do it right now – we have a special place, you know? Perfect for little scum like you. Where no one hears anything. And we will – if we want to – break every bone in your body.' He took me by the arm, and was squeezing it and lifting it. 'We will break this first. You understand that, don't you?'

I was nodding still, and shivering, and stinking. My twisted arm was in the air, me on my knees, and I waited for the snap, the pain so great I was silent, open-mouthed, unable to make a sound, just waiting.

'We could put you in the trash and nobody would care. Nobody would even come looking – you understand me? You'd end up in a sack.'

I nodded. I could not speak.

'So I'm going to ask you one last time . . .' He hoisted me and bent me over the window so I was staring down, and I felt someone take my ankles so all they had to do was tip me out. Again, I was looking at the ground as they balanced me. 'Where is the bag you found?'

I tried to look up, but my arm was so bent and my back was so twisted. I tried to speak, and couldn't, and tried again. I said, 'On my mother's soul, sir—'

The man shouted: 'What? I can't hear you!'

I was tipped out more, and I screamed for help. 'I promise, I promise!' I shouted. 'I found money only. I found no bag. If I had found it . . . if I knew anything about it, I swear you would have it now. I would give it to you! I would – please, listen . . .' I could hardly breathe but I found the words. 'I would take you back to my house and give it to you. But how can I, sir, when I did not find it?'

I started sobbing, because I knew that this was my last chance. I felt the hands on my ankles shift, and then – after some silence – I was lifted back into the room and dropped onto the floor.

When I looked up, I could see the men talking together in low voices. I was shaking all over, and I could not move. After more time, one of them looked over and told me to stand up.

'You've shat yourself, haven't you?' he said.

I nodded, and I clawed my way up the wall so I was half standing.

The man shook his head. 'You stink of it. And of garbage.' He turned away from me. 'We're wasting our time,' he said. 'Boy, that's all you are, that's what all of you are. You are a piece of garbage. What are you?'

'Sorry, sir, garbage, sir.' I whispered it.

'Eleven hundred pesos, wasting our time with crap. Look at you.'

I managed to meet his eyes again, waiting to be struck as he came over.

'What is the point of you, eh?' He turned to the other men. 'Look at him – why do these people keep breeding? Put your hands behind your back.'

I did so, and waited to be hit.

He sighed more heavily, and I could see that he hadn't slept for a long time – he was frightened and tired. I prayed in my head – I could see he was weighing me, looking me over, wondering what, if anything, I was worth. Valuable or trash? To be kept here and beaten and beaten . . . or thrown away? What if they brought Gardo? What if they brought my aunt, and beat three different stories out of us?

I think I held my breath.

At last he decided. He looked at the policeman behind me and said, 'Get him out. We're wasting time.'

I felt a hand on the back of my neck. I was taken out of the door. I was taken down the stairs, and a guard took me down a passage and down more steps. A few minutes later, I was on the street, and I found myself running on legs that bent like I was drunk, and wouldn't do as I wanted. But at least I was running, crazily, down a long, empty road. At least I was free, and at least – unlike poor José Angelico – I was alive.

My legs got stronger. I knew then that I could run for ever.

3

It was raining and cool.

I just kept running steadily. I had no idea where I was and I didn't care – I felt like I could run for ever. I ran through the streets, heading for any lights that I saw. I had no money at all, and I didn't care. The world felt so big, the rain was so fresh, and I remember thinking, *Why is it raining in the dry season? How can it be so cool?* The sky was so high. Time had slowed right down, but it can't have been more than three hours, and as I ran I realized more and more how stuck the police were, if I was the only clue they had. Again it was clear how important the things we'd found must be, and then I began to think how lucky I was and how close death had been.

The hand could have opened and dropped me. I could have been thrown away, I could be – now, right now – slowly dying on a stone floor.

I closed my eyes and ran faster with my arms stretched out.

My auntie had said, 'Raphael found something,' and that was the only clue they had. Just those words had led to the whole neighbourhood being searched, me being taken. Taken, but free now.

At last I slowed to a walk, and at the far end of the street I saw a landmark I knew. I didn't know its name, but I knew it was in the city business district. The landmark was the statue of a soldier, raised up high. He had a drawn sword, ready for some charge in some war. I had passed him before, yelling something to his comrades, fighting for freedom! I walked right up to him and looked up, and I said, 'They let me go. I did not give it up.'

I could not believe they had let me go, and the statue just carried on yelling.

There was a surge of rain and the kind of breeze I'd felt up on the dumpsite, in from the sea – a typhoon breeze, though this was not the typhoon season. I looked at the soldier and thought, *So, am I garbage?* And I laughed, because it occurred to me – there and then – that the garbage boy had just lied his way out from under the noses of those clever men. A little garbage boy had sat there shaking, saying, 'I don't have the bag,' when all the time I knew exactly where it was and what had been in it. We'd caught the train and we'd found the locker. We had the letter – and OK, we did not know what it all meant yet. But the garbage boys were way ahead of the garbage police, and I had said nothing to those men.

I walked on.

It would take two or three hours to reach Behala, and I was so happy walking – I knew which direction to take. I passed an old man and two little kids with a cart. They were night sweepers, shovelling trash. I asked the man if he had a cigarette, and he looked at me strangely. I had forgotten that my face was covered in blood.

He gave me a little bit of a cigarette, and I sat and smoked with him. The kids stood and looked at me, and I was stinking, but nobody seemed to care much. The little girl was about five, and the other – maybe a girl, maybe a boy – looked about seven. The seven-year-old got a bottle of water out of the cart, and I splashed some over my nose and mouth. Then I said goodbye and started running again.

Let me tell you something else – I think I will tell it now.

On that computer we had found out about José – the man whose bag it was. José Angelico, God rest his poor soul, was a dead man. His name had been in the news. Gardo had said, 'What if he's a killer?' – but it turned out the poor man had been killed.

Guess where he had died?

He had died in a police station. The newspaper said that he had died while police were interrogating him. In the same police station as me? I wondered. In the same room?

Had they dropped him from the window on purpose? By mistake?

I was passing a little park, and I ducked into it for a moment and sat on the grass. The rain was so light and cool. I guess I was in deep shock, so I just sat for a while, and I thought more about poor José Angelico.

He had been arrested on suspicion of a major, major crime – it had made all the papers. After the computer, we had gone to the papers – one thing there's a lot of on the dumpsite is old newspapers. It didn't take us long to find the right ones, and we sat there like three little old men, me reading it all out to Rat, who nodded and stared. The police had arrested José Angelico for robbery.

Six million dollars.

We sat back and tried to imagine what even a thousand dollars looks like. Gardo tried to translate it into pesos and got a headache so bad he had to lie down. We were laughing, trying to imagine how you walk with all those million dollars in your pocket, and then we stopped laughing.

José Angelico had died in a police station, they said, and that's why I stuck to the lie, even as they held me out of that window – for the sake of José Angelico and his serious-faced little girl. I also think José was with me, because I know the dead come back.

The crime he was accused of was robbing a government man – the vice-president – of six million dollars, and maybe he'd done it and the money was waiting somewhere. He must have put that bag in the trash before they got him – I think perhaps they made him confess to it, and that's when they came looking.

One newspaper told us a little bit about him. It said that he had been an orphan, but had been adopted by a man called Dante Jerome Olondriz, son of Gabriel Olondriz. That was the name on the letter we'd found – Gabriel Olondriz, the man in Colva Prison. José Angelico, it said, had worked as a houseboy for the vice-president for eighteen years. It said that José Angelico had an eight-year-old daughter and no other family. That was why he was writing to Gabriel Olondriz.

I sat shaking in the rain, and I knew for sure now that we would have to go to Colva Prison and deliver the letter.

4

My name is Grace and you will hear only one thing from me.

Father Juilliard has asked me to say what kind of a man José Angelico was, as I worked closely with him. I am a maid to Senator Zapanta – the vice-president who was robbed. I have been his maid for four years, so I knew the senior houseboy well. I can say that José was kind, gentle, trustworthy and honest. He had a very quiet voice. He didn't smoke. He took a little brandy at the weekend, but not so much. His wife had died before I knew him, and he was paying for his daughter to go to school. Her name was Pia Dante, but she could not live with her father. José was live-in staff, and the senator's house is a long way from schools. He boarded her with a family near to her school, and they saw each other once a week. He had also had a son, but the little boy had died very young.

I don't know what else to say.

I was very, very upset when I heard about it, and like everyone, I said it was impossible. José Angelico was the most trustworthy man, and he did not seem brave. As soon as I could – after he had been taken – I went to find his daughter. But when I found the house, I was told she had gone. I asked where, I asked when, and I honestly tried to find a way of looking for her – but the family that had boarded her were not helpful. I don't know what happened to the little girl. There are many boys and girls on the streets, as everybody knows.

José Angelico was a good man, whatever he did – and I won't forget him.

PART THREE

1

I'm Olivia Weston, and I was what they call a 'temporary house-mother' at Behala's Mission School. I also have one part of the story. The boys and Father Juilliard have asked that I write it down carefully, so that is what I will do.

I'm twenty-two, and I was taking time after university to see some of the world. I came to the city intending to stay in it for a few days, get over my jet-lag, and then fly on to meet up with friends for a month or so of swimming and surfing.

I visited the Behala dumpsite, though, and my plans changed.

I did go swimming and surfing – I did have a holiday. But I found lying on the beach was good for a week, and then I started to feel restless and useless. Behala had hit me hard, and I couldn't get it out of my mind. I'd gone there to deliver some sponsorship money for my parents, who had a friend who'd worked there. My father works in the Foreign Office, and had paid my airfare (and a bit more) in the hope I'd get something educational out of the trip. Sure enough, before I knew it, Father Juilliard had suggested I teach reading and writing to the little ones. Then I got involved in a water-sanitation project they have going. Then I was doing very basic first aid, because the kids are always getting scratched or bitten, and things go septic fast – and then I got the title 'temporary house-mother' – which means you agree to do daytime shifts helping out wherever you can.

I fell in love.

I fell in love with the eyes looking at me, and the smiles. I think charity work is the most seductive thing in the world, and I'd never done it before. For the first time in your life you're surrounded by people who tell you you're making a difference. The Behala children are beautiful, and to see them on the rubbish tips all day can break your heart. If you come to this country, do the tourist things. But come to Behala too and see the mountains of trash, and the children who pick over them. It is a thing to change your life.

I knew Jun – the little boy they called Rat. Jun would not call me Olivia – it was always 'Sister', and then it became 'Mother'. I am stupidly soft-hearted – I will drip tears over a stray cat back in England. Little Jun had me wrapped round his finger in about two days, and I was forever giving him little bits of food, and little bits of money. I don't know how else a boy like that survives.

We have a rest room in the school, where people can go when it all gets too much, and just lie down under a fan. We've got a small fridge in there too – and the house-mothers use it as a base. Jun got into the habit of visiting me and trying to make things tidy, and I got into the habit of giving him things. So when he brought his two friends to see me, it was a nice surprise but I had no idea what I was getting involved in.

They asked if we could talk, and I assumed it was about what had happened the night before. Father Juilliard was resting, and I didn't want to disturb him – he'd been up most of the night trying to find out where Raphael had been taken, and I think he was still badly shaken – the police had not been helpful. Then, of course, the child had simply come walking back to Behala, walking in as the sun rose. I wasn't there, but I'd heard all about it – and I could see how badly he'd been beaten. His auntie had held him and held him, and wouldn't let him go. The whole neighbourhood came out, apparently. Father Juilliard says the people here are like that. When one of their number is hurt, everyone feels the wound.

Now he smiled shyly at me, pulling back his hair. The bruising was terrible, and I remember wondering how an adult could possibly strike such a child. He saw me staring, and moved behind his friend. Gardo – the bald boy – put his hand very gently on his arm before turning back to me.

Jun said, 'We don't know what to do, Mother. We've got a big problem. You know Gardo, yes?'

Gardo sat down, looking at his knees. I could see that he had tried to dress up clean – he looked scrubbed and his T-shirt was fresh. He tried to smile, but he just looked nervous. I was jumping to the conclusion, of course, that he was about to ask for money – and I was bracing myself to refuse. One of Father Juilliard's rules was that we did not give money away as gifts. The odd ten or twenty, yes – everyone did a little bit of that now and then. But I knew Gardo was building up to ask for a big sum. I was surprised, then – and a bit ashamed – when he said, 'My grandfather's in prison, ma'am, and I want to go and see him.'

I said, 'I'm so sorry. Which prison?'

He told me the name, and as I knew nothing about the city's prisons it didn't mean much and I wondered why I'd asked the question.

'Why is he in prison?' I said.

Gardo looked away, and the bruised boy – Raphael – put his arm round his shoulders and said something in his own language. I realized I had touched on something personal, but I could hardly back-track now – and in any case, it was one of the logical questions.

'They say he beat up someone,' said Jun softly, 'but it's not true. It's all corruption because there's some men who want his house.'

Gardo, I saw, had started to cry. He wiped his eyes and said: 'They're trying to get him out of his house! They file a charge. They pay the police, the police arrest him. Now they've got his house.'

Gardo wiped tears away again. Raphael hugged him harder, and said something again – something reassuring, I assumed – in his own language.

Then he said to me: 'Gardo needs to see him, Sister.' The boy's mouth was swollen, and his speech was awkward. 'Can you help us get to the prison?'

I took a gulp of water, and Jun topped up my glass.

It was dawning on me that I had been right: this was going to be a request for money. They needed bus fares, or bribe money. I was surprised again, therefore, when Gardo said: 'We need you to go with me, Sister. Please?'

'Me?'

They all nodded.

'You want me to go and see your grandfather?' I said. Gardo nodded.

'How?' I said. I was completely bewildered. 'Why do I need to see him?'

'We've got to get some information to him,' said Gardo. 'The police were asking questions about him – that's why they beat my friend. Maybe they come for me next time!'

'I don't understand.'

'It's a difficult situation, Mother,' said Jun. I'd never seen him so grave. 'The old man needs to know what is going on here. We need some information too, to help him. Or he loses the house.'

'But your family, perhaps – your mother . . .'

Gardo shook his head. 'No mother.'

'Your grandfather must have sons,' I said. 'And there must be visiting times – why can't somebody just . . . visit? I'm not sure what good I can do, that's the problem.'

Gardo said, 'You don't understand.'

'You're right,' I said. 'I don't.'

'The prisons here,' said Jun. 'A visit once a month. Mother, they're going to lose their house – that's everything here. You lose your house, you've got nothing. And you – you're a social worker . . .'

Gardo said: 'You take your passport. You sign your name. They let you inside.'

I was silent. At last we'd got to the bottom of it.

The boy said something I didn't hear, and put his head in his hands. Jun put his hand on mine and said, 'We ask you because it is so important and no one else can help.'

'You're the only foreigner we know,' said Raphael. 'And the prisons out here . . . they do what they want.'

'You say you're a social worker,' said Jun. 'You say you just want to see him for half an hour. They may keep you waiting, OK? They may say no at first. But in the end, if you just sit there . . . There's a chance, yes?'

Gardo looked at me, and his eyes were still full of tears.

Jun said, 'You're the nicest, kindest mother we ever had here. He's only asking because, without this, they maybe gonna lose the house.'

'They beat me,' said Raphael. 'They think I got some papers, but I don't have them.'

'Please, Mother?'

That was how I found myself in a taxi heading for Colva Prison.

Vanity and stupidity, and the fact that three little boys could break my heart one minute and flatter me the next, all the time lying and lying. I took just Gardo with me, and the first thing we did was stop at a big store to get him some new clothes. He'd cleaned himself up, as I said, but his shorts and shirt were ingrained with so many months' dirt they were stiff on his body.

The looks I got walking him into the boys' clothing department were something I'll never forget. And the time it took him to choose was also something I remember. I'd asked the taxi to wait, thinking, *Shorts and a shirt – five minutes of shopping*. Unfortunately it wasn't like that. Gardo wanted to take his time, and he was the most intent, careful shopper I'd ever seen. He wanted jeans, and he wanted the most expensive kind. I could not pay western prices for something that I knew was probably made for peanuts in this very city, so I managed to talk him down to a cheaper pair. Then he wanted a long basketball shirt, which I thought was totally wrong for the impression we were hoping to create. I took him to a rack with formal shirts on it, and he turned his nose up at all of them. I was beginning to get flustered by now, so again we compromised. We chose a T-shirt, which he insisted must be too big. Then we chose a more formal shirt with a collar, to wear over the top.

He tried it all on, and we went to the checkout – or I thought we were heading that way, but suddenly I was in the shoe section, and he was looking at trainers. Again, the prices stunned me, but I had to admit that a smartly dressed boy with bare feet – dirty bare feet – is not going to be convincing.

We chose a medium-priced pair, and when we got to the checkout I put it all on my credit card. The reward, of course, was that I had never seen a boy so happy in my life, and – I have to say – so handsome. He emerged from the changing room, and he was simply no longer a Behala dumpsite boy! He was taller, he was bursting with confidence and smiles . . . he was even walking differently. I could not resist kissing him, which made the shop assistants howl with laughter.

We got to the taxi. I gulped when I saw the meter. And on we went.

2

Father Juilliard.

I feel I ought to say that had I known what Olivia had agreed to do, I would have intervened and prevented it. I would have seen it for the scam that it was. The problem is, you never see them coming, and six years here in Behala have taught me that some of our children are the best liars in the world. I guess it is survival. It's awful to say it, but . . . trust. You just shouldn't put yourself in a position where trust could be betrayed.

I am the worst, though. While they were working on Olivia, they had very special plans for me.

Raphael and Gardo were smart. But little Jun . . . Rat. What he did took my breath away.

Things were about to get very dangerous indeed.

3

Olivia. And yes, I know. It was stupid.

The taxi took me into a part of the city that was more squalid than I'd ever seen. You may say that's strange, coming from someone who works in Behala, but it's not. Behala is a huge, monstrous, filthy, steaming rubbish dump and you cannot believe human beings are allowed to work there, let alone live there. Rubbish and shacks – it's extreme, it's horrible and I will never forget the stink.

Behala also makes you want to weep, because it looks so like an awful punishment that will never end – and if you have any imagination, you can see the child and what he is doomed to do for the rest of his life. When you see the old man, too weak to work, propped in a chair outside his shack, you think, *That is Raphael in forty years. What could possibly change?* These children are doomed to breathe the stink all day, all night, sifting the effluent of the city. Rats and children, children and rats, and you sometimes think they have pretty much the same life.

Colva, however, was something else again.

We drove on cracked roads. The pavements were broken, and it looked as if there'd recently been an earthquake. We drove between low-rise flats, strewn with washing and electricity cables. There were people everywhere, mainly sitting as if they had nothing ever to do. The taxi's air-con wasn't working, and it was getting hotter and hotter. This was the dry season, but there was talk of a freak typhoon coming in from the sea. There was real heat in the breeze.

We turned, and on our right was a high concrete wall. Gardo said, 'Prison,' and pointed, but you did not need to be told. There were coils of barbed wire at the top, some of it straggling down where it had come loose from its moorings. There were guard towers every fifty paces, open to the sun and rain. We turned right and followed the next wall. On the left were huts of bamboo and straw, and more people – many of them tiny children. I always notice the tiny children, sitting in the dirt, playing with stones and sticks. I learned later that many of the families in these shacks had relatives as inmates on the other side of the wall. They had to live there and get food in, or the prisoner would starve.

We came round to the entrance and I paid off the taxi. Then I walked up to the guardhouse. It was a concrete box with a large window. Several guards sat inside. Beside it was a red and white barrier to stop vehicles, and a man with a machine gun. I showed my passport and delivered the speech I had prepared.

They made a phone call. I noticed that Gardo was holding my hand, and I too was scared. We were kept waiting for no more than two minutes, and another officer came to the window and asked me to repeat what it was I wanted. I told the story twice because another person arrived, and then my passport was taken away. I was given a register to sign, and a visitor badge. Gardo got one too. Then we were led round the barrier and across a yard.

To walk into a prison is a very frightening thing, because you cannot help but think, *What if something goes wrong and they won't let me out?* I was also thinking about that line – the line there has to be, and you have to cross – that separates freedom from complete incarceration. What door would it be that would swing open and shut again behind us?

We were taken past an office, and to what looked like a large waiting room. There were benches all the way round it, and we were invited to sit. Seconds later, a guard came to escort us out of the waiting room, down a corridor. At the end of the corridor was an iron gate made of bars. It was unlocked for us, and we all walked through, and it closed with that dreadful, clanging, ringing slam of metal on metal. We were shown to a smaller waiting room and asked to sit. We sat there for nearly an hour.

You don't get anywhere in this country by showing impatience – I learned that very quickly here. It is so much better to wait, and smile, and nod. Gardo said almost nothing. I could see his lips moving, as if he was saying a prayer.

Out of the blue, he said to me, 'What is *in memoriam?'*

I said, 'I think it's Latin. When somebody dies, you write that and it means, "in memory of".' I asked him why he wanted to know.

He smiled at me and said, 'Video game.' Then he started muttering again, as if he was reciting the same long prayer.

Eventually the door opened and a man in a short-sleeved shirt came in. He had a very warm smile, and he shook my hand and introduced himself as Mr Oliva. I told him my name was Olivia, and it seemed to break the ice instantly. He assured me that Mr Oliva would help Miss Olivia if he possibly could. He had a photocopy of my passport in his hand, and he sat opposite me.

He was quietly spoken and so polite, and apologized for keeping me waiting.

'I'm the social welfare officer,' he said. 'The governor is busy with some problems at the moment, or he would see you himself – we always try to accommodate these requests. The inmate you wish to see, he does get these requests quite often. You've given us his number, but it's not the right number. Are you quite sure it's Mr Olondriz that you want to see?'

'I think so,' I said.

'Yes, please, sir,' said Gardo. 'Gabriel Olondriz.'

'Like I say, he does get visitors and is always keen to see them. You know he's a very sick man?'

Gardo nodded at me, and I said: 'Yes.'

There was a silence.

'It's one of the reasons we're here,' I said.

'It is not out of the question,' said Mr Oliva. 'There are some formalities, however. Usually we can set these things up all the better if we have some notice, you see. You could come next week maybe?'

I shook my head. 'I'm very sorry,' I said. I could feel Gardo's panic – he could sense we were close to success. 'I'm embarrassed, in fact. This is my friend Gardo, and he only told me about the problems yesterday, and he says it's urgent. I think it's incredibly kind of you to even consider seeing us.'

Mr Oliva smiled. 'You are very patient and very educated. You're a social worker, yes? In Behala?'

'I'm an unpaid worker – it's completely voluntary.'

Mr Oliva extended his hands and shook mine firmly. 'Thank you,' he said. 'Without people coming to help like this, things would be worse than they are. This city has many problems. Every city has problems – but maybe this city has more than most, I don't know. You are looking after this boy?'

I said, 'He was very upset yesterday. I didn't understand everything, but he told me I might be able to do something.'

'Is he a good boy?'

'Yes.'

'He goes to your school?'

'Not as often as I would like,' I said, and Mr Oliva laughed.

He exchanged a few words with Gardo and patted his arm. 'You know the man you wish to see is in the hospital at the moment?'

'I don't know very much about him,' I said, 'except what Gardo told me.'

'He's not a well man. I think you might be upset. Also, the conditions – the meeting area. You've been in a prison before?'

I shook my head.

Mr Oliva smiled. 'You see, our government has many pressing problems. It does not put money into its prisons – I think the same was true in your country a hundred years ago. I think you will be upset by what you see. Perhaps just the boy should come – if it's between him and Mr Olondriz?'

'I think I ought to be with him,' I said.

I didn't know why. I was getting frightened again – but having come this far, would I really sit in the waiting room? This was my year of seeing the world, and it occurred to me that to see the world of Behala, and now a jail – perhaps it would teach me more than I'd ever found at university.

Mr Oliva said, 'The problem is the fees. To organize visits like this – to "fast-track", so to speak. They told you at the gate?'

'They didn't,' I said.

'They were embarrassed,' he replied. 'It is a question of getting security clearance – we have to send somebody very fast for approval. We could get a waiver if you gave us some time.' He looked so honest. 'Is it really so urgent?' he said.

I nodded.

'I can check in a moment,' he said. 'But I think it will be ten thousand. And a receipt – with the governor so busy . . .'

'I don't need a receipt,' I said. I must admit, I felt slightly sick. The day was costing me a fortune. 'The problem is, I'm not sure I'm carrying as much as that.'

Gardo was looking away.

'I'll get the forms and check,' Mr Oliva said. 'I want very much to help you, but . . . I don't set the fees, they are set by the government.' He smiled. 'I think the government must be very rich!'

Ten minutes later he was back. He had a form in his hand. 'You will have to be photographed also, I'm afraid. And I was right: it is ten thousand.'

I was carrying eleven thousand. I had been to the bank that morning and had withdrawn extra because I was meeting friends for dinner in a very expensive restaurant that night. In half an hour they'd made a security pass for me, with my photograph and a number of signatures. Mr Oliva shook my hand again.

As he left, he called out loudly, and in a moment there were four guards in the corridor. One said something to Gardo, and he said, 'Come.'

I remember their echoing boots.

We were led to another room with lockers. We were asked to take everything out of our pockets – we had to take off our shoes and shake them. They put everything inside and slammed the locker doors, and we set off down another passageway, and I could hear people in the distance, shouting – I knew the dividing line was close now, and my heart was beating fast. Sure enough, the corridor took us into a long hall, bisected by floor-to-ceiling bars, and the shouting of men was louder still, as if we were coming to some kind of market place. We were led to a gate in the centre, and as the guards opened it, I became aware of the constant banging of metal on metal. Everywhere, doors were slamming, and I could hear the ratcheting of keys in locks. Suddenly we were in a strange no-man's-land, like a decompression chamber – a space in which the door behind us locked before the door in front was opened. Under all the shouting there was laughter, and – I have to say it – it was like animal noise, with a dreadful echo. It was also, if it were possible, getting hotter, as if something was breathing on us. Orders were shouted: everyone was suddenly in a hurry. That final door was unlocked, and we were beckoned through.

'Welcome!' cried the guard receiving us.

He smiled at me. A smile of genuine interest and warmth, which seemed so wrong for the hell we were walking into.

4

I had expected cells, but all I saw was cages.

They were on my left and right, and they were the type of cages you might put lions and tigers in, in an old-fashioned zoo. They were just high enough for a short man to stand up in, and they were about four metres long, maybe two metres deep. I looked up and saw that these cages were stacked three high, with ladders up the sides. They continued in long rows, and I could see that there were alleyways between them. It was so terribly hot. As we passed the alleyways, I saw that they led you deep into more cages. It was like a warehouse, but every cage held people.

As I walked among them, I was being stared at from left and right, and from above. Also, because many people were lying down or sitting, I was being stared at from below.

The noise was impossible – everyone seemed to be shouting. Gardo put his hand in mine again and it steadied me.

'Hello, ma'am!' was being shouted, again and again. Cheerful cries – friendly cries, and so much laughter. There were hands stretching out between the bars, and there were solemn faces as well as the laughing faces.

'Can you spare something, ma'am? Ma'am! Ma'am! How are you? How are you?'

I looked to the right and stopped dead.

I was looking at a boy who could not have been more than eight years old, wearing only shorts. He was smiling at me. In his lap sat a younger boy, sleeping.

I think I said, 'No,' and just looked at him, unable to move – stuck for a moment.

Gardo eased me forward gently, but the eight-year-old started calling eagerly, and he stood up and came to the front of the cage so that he was holding the bars with both hands. 'Hello, ma'am!' he said. 'Hello, ma'am – twenty pesos, ma'am.'

I turned round in a full circle. I was in the centre of the place by now, and to turn was to lose yourself, because all the cages were identical, and though there were big signs with numbers, they meant nothing to me. I had no sense of direction any more: all I could see was faces and hands waving. Man then child. Young man, then older man, then child again – thin bodies, glistening with sweat. Almost everyone in shorts only, and a smell of old food, sweat and urine.

'It's OK,' said Gardo, keeping his hand over mine.

The guard who was escorting us had not noticed that we'd stopped. Now he did, and waited. I was being asked questions. 'Where are you going? Where are you going, Sister?'

'What's your name?'

'What country?'

'American? American? Hi there!'

'I love you! I love you, Joe!'

The guard came back. Gardo had my hand and my arm, and was trying to get me moving. It was oven-hot, and the smell was getting worse. I knew that if I didn't move, I would fall. I had a water bottle with me, thank goodness – and I drank deep and long, and there were people cheering. People were shouting out for water. I lost my balance and staggered against bars – Gardo was there, but he couldn't hold me. I felt hands on my arm and on my hair, and voices whispering close:

'Help me, ma'am . . .'

'Nobody here, ma'am – nobody coming, ma'am . . .'

There was a young boy with dyed hair lying back in the arms of an older man; there was a child in a pair of torn pants curled up on a piece of newspaper. They were living in a furnace.

Gardo disentangled the hands – they were stroking me. Anxious eyes, still so well-mannered – even in despair, to keep your manners – I could feel tears, useless tears rising in my stupid eyes.

I managed to walk on. It was like going uphill – I managed to take one step, then another, and as if I was on stepping stones, I continued up the corridor. I looked ahead, at the guard's blue-shirted back, and followed him, and we came to a metal door and went through it. When it shut behind me, I leaned against the wall and closed my eyes and cried.

There was a staircase, and when I had recovered, I went up it. The noise and the smell gradually faded from me.

The guard said, 'He is in the hospital now.'

He said something to a second guard, and another door was unlocked for us. We moved out of the bright light, and I was aware of a breeze from a wall fan. My eyes took time to adjust, because the light was dim. I was led along a narrow corridor – I think there was a wheelchair. Then I was taken to the right, into an empty room, and there was a table, and several folding chairs. I sat in one and put my head low down, because I still felt that I might pass out. I think Gardo disappeared for a moment – I think I was left alone. I drank more water, and after some time I felt better.

Gardo reappeared and sat next to me.

I said, 'There were children in there.'

Gardo just looked at me.

'What have they done?'

He shrugged. 'They're poor. They do many things.'

'But . . . you can't lock people up like that. What have they done?'

Gardo said nothing. 'They steal,' he said, after some time. 'Maybe fighting.' He smiled his thin smile, as if to encourage me. 'They get some food. It's not so bad.'

We waited for . . . I don't know – time had changed. Maybe not long. And then we heard voices, and two guards arrived. They were helping a very old man towards us. They had to be slow and patient with him, because he could not walk very well. He was wearing dark, loose-fitting trousers and a white shirt, buttoned at the neck. The guards supported him, but I saw that he had a stick as well, and he made his way painfully along the passage. He was staring at me, and I was struck by his burning white eyes – short-sighted, but hungry – peering, as if he had been waiting for me.

5

Olivia still. They asked me to write all of this but maybe Gardo needs to say things as well. I noticed that he – Gardo, I mean – had stood up and moved behind me. I stood up too. Nobody seemed quite sure what to do.

'Miss Olivia?' said the man.

'Yes,' I said.

He blinked. 'Sit. Please, sit.' Then he said something in his own language, and the guards helped him to the chair. He was perspiring heavily – I could see moisture all over his forehead, and he found a handkerchief and mopped first his brow, and then his face, and then his neck.

At last he sat back and smiled. 'They told me your name,' he said. 'Thank you so much for visiting me. I hope it hasn't been too . . . dreadful for you.'

It was clearly an effort for him to speak. He seemed very sick to me – far too sick to be in prison. I couldn't think of anything to say.

'I do not *recognize* your name,' he continued. 'And nobody would tell me the reason for . . . paying me this honour. Please . . . forgive me, I'm . . . As you can see, you've come when I'm extremely weak. But I never say no. I never say no.'

The man was not simply weak: he was dying. I don't know how I knew, but I was certain of it. His skin was drawn tight, and breathing was so hard. There was a large growth under his jaw, and he seemed to be in pain. Everything was an effort. Sitting still was an effort, and lifting his head was an effort – I saw him wince as he adjusted his position. He smiled at me again, and I saw his skull clearly through the skin. This was Gardo's . . . grandfather? But something didn't seem right. The man had not even greeted him.

'I'm pleased to meet you,' he said. 'I will tell you anything you want to know. What is your brief?'

I still hadn't spoken, and I wasn't sure that I could. I wasn't sure what my voice would sound like if I did. I moistened my lips and said: 'I'm so sorry to have . . .' I couldn't think what to say. 'To have . . . disturbed you. But Gardo . . .'

I looked round and Gardo was standing there, still as a post. He had not greeted the man, and the man had still not greeted him.

'Believe me,' said the old man, 'a visitor is always welcome. Without visitors I would have gone mad, and they come in fits and starts. I can go several weeks with nobody. Then it is as if I am back in fashion: I have two in a day. You, my dear, are the first face for some time. And your boy, this is . . . ?'

'This is Gardo,' I said. 'You know each other, don't you?'

The old man looked at me and then at Gardo. He seemed puzzled, and he smiled.

'You do know each other,' I said. 'It's actually Gardo who wants to see you. About your house.'

The man said something in his own language, and Gardo replied softly. The man spoke again, and Gardo said nothing.

'Miss Olivia,' said the old man, smiling. He closed his eyes and waited. 'I'm sure your boy is a good boy, and I am delighted that he's brought you here. But to answer your question . . .' He paused again, this time for breath. 'To answer your question: no. I am not acquainted with him and I have never seen him before. As for a house . . . I have no house. I have almost nothing. It was all taken from me a long time ago.'

'Gardo, you said this was your grandfather,' I said.

Gardo was looking away.

'I don't understand,' I said. 'You told me . . . Sir, I'm a bit confused.'

'Yes. So am I.'

'The reason I came was . . . I just said it: Gardo wanted to see you about your house.'

I was going over Gardo's story in my mind, and the confusion was getting worse and making me panic. Was it the wrong prisoner? There had been confusion over the number. Were we sitting with the wrong man?

'Olivia, you don't know who I am, do you? You don't know anything about me.'

'No,' I said. 'I have no idea.'

He said something to Gardo in his own language, and Gardo answered softly.

The man drew breath sharply, and closed his eyes. 'He says you paid ten thousand pesos to get to me. He is very generous with your money, I think. The going rate, Miss Olivia, is fifteen hundred. They got five thousand from a journalist once, but they kept him waiting three days and it was coming up to the Zapanta election.'

'I don't understand,' I said. 'Do you know Gardo or not?'

'No.'

'Then . . .'

'He has used you to bribe his way to me. The money you paid bribes the administration here. The guards will bring people to me, and – like I said – there are often people wanting to see me, and I thought you must be one of them. The prison authorities make a good living from me, I think.'

'But I don't . . . I still don't understand. Why do people come to see you?'

'Gardo, you're not going to explain this?'

Gardo said something in his own language, and there was a short, abrupt exchange. Gardo seemed to be pleading, but the old man interrupted. 'No,' he said.

'No. We speak in English with Miss Olivia. Miss Olivia has paid for this interview. We will say everything in English.' He looked at me. 'Your boy is playing a game and he wants to ask me questions on his own. He wants to speak to me privately, and I have said no. I can see you are bewildered, and – I am also very surprised . . . please.'

He bent forward in his chair, and I thought for a terrible moment he was going to be sick. He leaned on his stick, and seemed to be waiting for the pain to pass. He said something to Gardo in his own language again. Gardo took a cup from the table and filled it from my water bottle. He handed it to the old man, but the old man was shaking. He got a hand to the cup, but Gardo had to keep hold of it and feed it gently up to his mouth. The man clutched the boy's arm.

'I'm sorry,' he said. He drank again. 'I was saying . . . If I tell you who I am, Miss Olivia, and how I come to be here, things may become clearer. I am very near death now, as you can see. Do you know they still will not let me out? As if I could harm a fly.' He smiled at me. 'You know my name, but it means nothing to you. There's no reason why it should.'

The pain had passed, and he was relaxing.

'The reason I am in this jail is that I brought corruption charges against Senator Regis Zapanta thirty-five years ago. Do you know Senator Zapanta?'

'No,' I said.

'He's a big man in this country – our trusted vice-president. He is always in the papers for one thing or another. You are a tourist and you're passing through – you would not know these names. Gardo here will know the name and even the face – is that true, Gardo?'

Gardo was nodding. 'Everyone knows him.'

'In this city he is a very big man. You don't read the papers?'

I shook my head.

'Nor do I any more. Once a month if I am lucky – they starve me of the news, and perhaps it's for the best. Waiting for change has exhausted me: it's probably best I hear so little! I was never important, Olivia – I served as a small officer only, in the east quarter of the city – humble ranks. You won't know the system, so I won't . . . Oh, it doesn't even matter. What matters is that forty years ago I came upon information that Senator Zapanta had spirited away thirty million dollars of international aid money. It was a package of grants, with the United Nations leading, and it was to build hospitals and schools. They called it "seed-corn" money. Now, "seed-corn" money is very important in the way these things work. When a country receives such money, it is a condition that a proportion of the money is matched by the government, and by other donor countries too. In this case, that thirty million was going to be added to, by our government here and by, oh . . . private investment – the big banks were involved. So that thirty would, we hoped, turn to sixty or seventy. Seventy million would have changed the city, Miss Olivia – at that time. But no schools or hospitals were ever built, and the city stayed poor. Senator Zapanta stole it, and I tried to prove he stole it. It never went to court, because the senator quickly counter-sued. It seemed he had many more friends than I, and infinitely more power. I ended up charged and prosecuted. I was convicted – my appeals were laughed at. Life imprisonment, I got, and . . .'

He paused again, and winced with pain.

'I think the sentence is nearly over.'

6

Gardo again – just something short from me. Just to say to Sister Olivia that I am so sorry for what I did. We talked about it, the three of us, and we decided it was the only way – Rat said maybe we could tell you part of it, but I said no. I was the one who said we should trust nobody but ourselves.

I am sorry for that.

You must remember, please, that it was I who read the letter from José Angelico, over and over and over. We all knew – all of us – that we were so close, and what Raphael went through in the police station . . . Sister, I do not know how he went through that. I thought he was soft before that, just a little boy who would break, but I was wrong. Please understand, we could not tell you. It was just the three of us: Raphael, Rat and me, and already we knew that soon we would be leaving – that it was not possible to stay much longer in Behala. So we did not want anyone to know anything.

Please forgive me for that, and I hope I see you again sometime. I am sorry how it ended for you.

7

Gabriel Olondriz smiled at me.

This is Olivia again.

'I will tell you a little more,' he said. 'It will make sense, in time, and then this boy will tell us what he wants.'

I said, 'How can a man steal thirty million dollars?'

'How?'

'Yes.'

'It is done so often. It is done so easily – not in a suitcase: it is not like robbing a bank. In the government's case it is usually done through bogus contracts: everybody siphons a little bit here, a little bit there. It is done through clever accounting and paying off the people who should be watching. In the case of Mr Zapanta, I know many men were involved, and some probably thought they were doing our country a service. It took me the best part of two years, but I assembled the paperwork. Like you, Miss Olivia, for some time I worked unsalaried, because this was volunteer work I deemed to be of very great importance. We got copies of false contracts, and the bank transfers to invented accounts. We got copies of transactions, always cash withdrawals, because this man always loved to handle cash. Huge sums in dollars!

Dollars were the currency, never our own – and where were they going? Olivia, forgive me. I have told this tale so often it no longer has any . . . freshness.'

'What happened?' I said.

'He was stock-piling dollars in a vault in his home.'

'But you . . . you couldn't prove it?'

'I had so much evidence. Unfortunately for me, I was naïve. My office was raided. The same night there was a terrible fire at my house. I was away, but both my maid and my driver were killed in it. And every scrap of evidence went up in smoke. Then, Olivia – this was the clever part. He had been planning my downfall, and charges were ready to be laid against me – for financial malpractice. It was suggested that I had defrauded the government of half a million dollars, and it was proved that I had organized the murder of a well-known banker. Miss Olivia . . . to learn about the crimes I had committed while . . . sleeping! At first I thought it was all so crazy, and all so obvious, that I need not be afraid. I had lawyers who were relaxed also, and sure of success. But the lawyers – I realized this way too late – had been bought, and they fed all my defence straight back to Mr Zapanta. It is enough to make you laugh, almost. The senator was smart. I was stupid. In this country you pay for being stupid, just as you pay for being poor. After a few months, just as the case was going well and I was certain to win it . . . I was arrested. Like I said, I was convicted.' He paused. 'I have been in jail ever since.'

Gardo stood up and pressed a cloth to the old man's forehead. I saw the old man hold Gardo's hand again.

'Please, sir,' said Gardo suddenly. 'Who is Dante Jerome?'

The old man looked at Gardo, and then at me.

'I think this boy has many questions,' he said. 'He has come to ask me questions, and I will answer them. Dante Jerome was my son.'

'What is the harvest?' said Gardo. 'Also – sir – there are some words: *It is accomplished*. What does this mean?'

The old man said: 'What is accomplished? What do you mean?' He was speaking quietly.

'It is accomplished,' said Gardo. *'Go to the house now, and your soul would sing.'*

The old man worked his lips, and stared. 'I need you to tell me what is accomplished,' he said. 'You have to explain yourself, I think.'

'I don't know,' said Gardo. 'I don't know what it means. But I am told that if you could visit Senator Zapanta's house right now, your soul would sing because it is accomplished.'

The old man opened his mouth, but he said nothing. He looked at me, and then at Gardo. His eyes had become luminous again, and he was leaning forward in his chair. He took hold of Gardo's wrist and said – very softly: 'Who are you, boy? Please stop playing games now. You know things that are very important.'

'I am from Behala dumpsite.'

'Yes. A street boy, I knew it.'

He held Gardo tight. 'And that is one of the . . . darkest streets, I think. I worked for many years with street children, my son also. You will think I am being cruel, Olivia, but under these new clothes I can smell the street. It never, ever goes away. Why are you here, boy? Please tell me.'

Gardo said: 'Because I have found a letter from Mr José Angelico, sir. We found it in a station locker. It is a letter that the police are looking for, and it is addressed to you, and it says that you must rejoice because it is accomplished.'

'Give me the letter.'

'I did not dare to bring it, sir.'

'Why not?'

'For fear it would be taken, sir.'

'José writes to me each year. Why would you have a letter he wrote to me?'

'We think he wrote it just before the police took him. We found it, and—'

'Why did the police take him? Where is he?'

'The police killed him, sir. He was killed when they were questioning him.'

Gardo spoke softly, but the last words still fell like a blow. I saw the old man wince again and buckle, and Gardo stood back from him. He talked softly to the old man in his own language, and the man seemed to take yet more blows – I watched his old hands clench into fists. When the gentleman looked up, his face was wet and all I could see was pain.

We watched the old man shake. Something deep inside was shaking him, and there was nothing we could do but watch.

8

This is me, Raphael.

Sister Olivia was a good friend to us that day, and – for reasons that will be clear soon enough – we did not see her again to say thank-you. Writing this is a way to say thank-you, and one day maybe we will meet again and say it the way we need to say it.

I am so sorry for deceiving you, Sister.

I must talk about what we did while Gardo was in the jail – which was important. Then I will hand over to Rat, and write for him. You see, he and I decided to do something too, because it was hard sitting waiting and waiting all day, and I have not felt right since the police station – I cannot stay still, and everyone is looking at me always. We took the letter again, and stole off by the canal to a place nobody goes – a place I felt safe in, where you could see people coming. We squatted down and went over the newspaper cuttings again, me reading them out, all the way through. I read the letter too, which was coming apart in my hands by now. We both knew it almost by heart, since we'd been helping Gardo remember it – even the jumble of numbers stuck on at the end. Those names again, coming at us: José

Angelico, the man killed in a police station. He felt like a brother to me now and I was dreaming about him. Gabriel Olondriz, his friend in Colva Prison. And now the fat senator, Zapanta . . . When I read the line about Senator Zapanta, Rat stopped me and made me re-read it: *If only you could go to Zapanta's house now: it would make your soul sing.*

'What's that mean?' said Rat.

I didn't know. We'd all been saying that every time we read it: *I don't know, don't know, don't know.*

'Where's his house, though? Maybe we should visit.'

'Green Hills,' I said. 'Everyone knows that. Same place as José Angelico.'

The senator was a famous man, and everyone knew he had a place out there, just beyond the city, big as a town. Everyone knew he was rich and old, and I'd seen his fat face in the papers I hooked up, oh, so often – papers that more often than not wrapped up the stupp. Everyone knew he owned big pieces of the city – there are only five or six families who do out here, and his name was on streets, on a shopping mall in the fancy part of town, and in rising skyscrapers . . . He was a big man in every way. Vice-president for two years and his smiling face everywhere.

It was Rat's idea to pay him a visit, and I liked the idea, if only to get me out of Behala.

'Why would seeing the place make your soul sing?'

said Rat. We wondered and wondered, and agreed that taking a trip might tell us.

It seemed to me the problem would be the usual one. Money – for the bus. I'd given everything to my auntie, so I was broke again.

Rat said to me, 'It's OK. I got enough.'

I have to say I didn't believe him. I said, 'How have you got anything?' I didn't say it to be mean – it's just that he's about the poorest-looking boy on the dumpsite, so the idea he had more than a peso made me smile.

He smiled right back at me and shook his head. 'I've got more than you think,' he said slowly. 'Come with me, and let's see who's poor.'

And that was when I came to learn a few things about Rat that I had never known and never asked about.

We cut back to the trail that takes you to the disused belt – belt number fourteen – checking the whole way that nobody was watching. I was still feeling scared whatever I did now – I could not shake it off, and I was always watching behind me, so when we went down the steps, and the rats flew up, I cried out and he had to hold me like a little kid.

'How do you live down here?' I said. It was the most disgusting place on the whole dumpsite.

He just laughed. 'It's the best house I ever had,' he said. 'You don't like it because you're lucky. You always had a house.'

'I don't know how you stand it, boy.'

'They don't bother me, I'm telling you. You get some that are friendly.'

'And what about at night?' I said. 'They never take a bite out of you?'

Rat laughed at me. 'They have a sniff, OK – maybe, when I'm sleeping. But what they gonna bite? There's no meat on me.'

He lit a couple of candles. I could hear scufflings in the wall, and mewling yelps.

'There's a nest somewhere,' I said. 'I wouldn't sleep down here if you paid me.'

'There's always nests everywhere. That's a big one, though, OK? They kept me awake last night – must be hundreds of them. Oh, and by the way – that bag . . .'

'What about it?'

Just the thought of the bag and I froze up.

'You can tell the police to come down here and look, because that bag's gone, Raphael. Two nights, and they'd eaten it. The wallet too: chewed up and disappeared.'

He was rocking a brick backwards and forwards gently. Then he turned and looked at me, suddenly serious.

'By the way,' he said, 'I better trust you. I just better trust you, and you better be good to trust. I know you're going to tell Gardo, but you tell nobody else!'

'Tell what?' I said. I had no idea what he was saying.

'I'm just thinking, here you are – here's me, showing you all my secrets. You could rob me blind now, you and Gardo – what would I do then?'

He was fierce, but all I could do was laugh at him. Not to be mean – but the idea of robbing Rat was crazy.

'What is there to rob?' I said. 'A little pair of shorts, and you're wearing them.'

Rat started to laugh right back at me. It was a high-pitched squeak of a laugh. The brick was on the floor now, and he was reaching into the space behind. Carefully, with his thin fingers – with the rats going crazy all around us – he removed a small metal box, not much bigger than a cigarette carton, and closed up tight. He set it between his feet and opened it.

He grinned up at me. 'Not much to rob, huh? You want to see what I've got? I've got more than you think.'

'What's in there?'

'Buried treasure, boy. Two thousand, three hundred and twenty-six pesos. My going-away fund.'

Sure enough, he showed it to me, counting it out. I think the amazement must have shown in my face, because he started laughing again, and rocking on his heels. 'I got one more box for just day-to-day stuff,' he said. 'One more tin box, that is, so the rats don't eat it. Two hundred and sixty in that one. I figure, today we're on a kind of holiday – so I'm gonna borrow out of this one, the travelling box.'

'But how do you get so much?' I said. I was totally amazed. Two thousand was a fortune for boys like us.

'I get it slow, and I keep it. Everyone gives me a little. The little piles up, and I don't eat much, or I get given food. Sister Olivia, for instance – she gave me fifty just yesterday, and then I went back for a sandwich.'

'And what are you saving for?'

Rat put his head down and seemed to be thinking hard. Then he crept to the steps and took a long look up them, like he really thought there might be someone listening. He came back and squatted – put a banknote in his pocket and closed the lid of the box. Then he put his hands up on my shoulders and looked right in my eyes.

'You and me are friends now,' he said, 'right?'

I nodded.

'Real friends?' he said.

'Of course,' I said.

'OK, I'm going to tell you something I never told any other boy. I told Olivia, made her promise to tell no one, just because I was so tired of never telling.' He dropped his voice to a whisper. A rat ran over his foot in the darkness, right between us; I had to force myself to keep still. 'I'm not from round here,' he said. 'You know that, don't you? Like, most of you are Behala boys, but I come from the south. I was at Central Station for nearly a year, and I heard about the Mission School, so this is where I came.'

I nodded again, and he was quiet. Like the secret inside was so big he couldn't say it.

'I want to go home, Raphael,' he said. He was so quiet I could hardly hear. 'I came off the islands when I had to. I want to go back.'

'Where's your home?'

'Sampalo. That's where I was born.'

'Go home then,' I said. 'You can go home with two thousand, can't you? The ferries cost . . . I don't know—'

He snorted, and I shut up.

'I can go home on the ferry, sure – go tomorrow if I want. And then what, when I get there? It's cost a thou just for the ticket. What happens then? You think people in Sampalo live on sand? That's why everybody comes *here*, man – that's why I came here. That's why I got sent here! I've gotta make a stake. Fifty thousand is what I need. Then I buy a boat, and I go home and fish for ever.'

'You can fish?' I said.

'Course I can fish! I was fishing before I could talk! I could swim before I could crawl! I will buy a boat, and I'm going to fish and fish and fish.'

I looked at Rat then, because he sounded so fierce – and that wide-eyed, old little face looked back at me. I tried to imagine him back on his island, Sampalo, steering his fishing boat, throwing out the lines. I'd heard of the place, of course – and never known it was Rat's home. It was a place people talked about, and I knew it was a long, long way away. Tourists went there, and it was supposed to be beautiful as paradise. You cried when you got there, you cried when you left – that's what people said.

'With a boat I can fish,' he said. 'That's got to be better than what we do here, hasn't it? Huh? Little house on the beach?' He was looking at me hard. 'Fishing boat out on the sand? None of this stink – none of this . . . crazy way to make a living. You, me. Gardo too – all of us maybe. Sun comes up, we're already out. Been out all night maybe – you think about it.'

'I can't fish,' I said.

'So what?' he said. 'I teach you. Cook what you need, sell the rest at the market – grow flowers. I had a sister grew flowers right out of the sand. You like the thought of that?'

'We'd need more money,' I said. 'We'd need to buy three boats, not one.'

'Yes,' said Rat. 'Maybe so. But . . .'

He was quiet a moment, thinking hard. 'Whatever happens, we can't stay here much longer, can we?'

I felt him touch my face very softly.

'I don't know,' I said. 'I guess we've got to wait and see what happens.'

'You can't stay here, Raphael. You'll always be thinking they're coming back for you.'

I was still swollen up and bruised, but the cuts were healing. My ribs were aching from when they hauled me in back through the window, and every time I touched them I felt sick again. So, yes – I did know what he meant, but how he knew it I don't know. That time with the police had changed everything, and people seemed different now too – people were looking at me strangely, like I'd brought bad luck. They'd all been pleased to see me back safe – but . . . my auntie was scared, and I was scared. There was something else too that I never told Rat, because I was ashamed.

It was sleep.

I was finding sleeping hard. I was having nightmares and waking up crying. I'll tell the truth – I said I would – I was wetting myself too. I would wake up with Gardo holding me like I was a baby and the cousins waking up scared, crying out, and the neighbours banging the walls because I was screaming so loud.

I think Auntie wanted me out, and I didn't know what to do about it.

9

This is Rat, also known as Jun-Jun – I tell my story and it's written down!

We took a bus from the dumpsite, took it right into the city to the big crazy bus station, Raphael going first and doing the talking. OK, he was bruised up, so he still looked a state – but when you look like me, you can't even get a ride very often, not when you're alone: you get kicked off like you're a curse. So he led the way but I was steering, hiding my ugly face till we were squeezed on up the back.

Of course, when we got to the stand we found out that buses to Zapanta's land went from a different place, so we jogged a couple of miles and caught a big red one. Under bridges, over bridges, me by the window looking out over the freeway past some shopping mall the size of a town with a great big sports stadium where they were going to have some great big boxing match, pictures of the fighters on scaffolds, grinning down like giants. People getting up and people getting down, running for the bus, and the ticket boy banging the side, screaming – then in two hours we were free and running out into the fruit fields in the sun. We went high up a hill and then came down into a valley, and it felt good to be getting so far away, and I could feel Raphael relaxing too, and we were humming to the music and playing with some sweet little kid on the seat in front of us. We even got a nice view of the sea, because Green Hills is right by a very pretty stretch. The rich all love a bit of the sea, don't they? – and it sure smells nicer than the sludge and stupp we call Behala.

Then the driver stopped by a huge set of gates and whistled to us.

People watched us getting down, and I said goodbye to them all, shaking hands for fun – them thinking I was a mad kid being taken out by a friend so smiling back. I was laughing when we hit the ground, and I took care that we moved on straight away, though I took a big look at the gatehouse – I wasn't going to let Raphael keep still, because I knew he was scared of everything, and if I let anything happen, Gardo would probably just cut my head off with his hook.

Two guards by the gate looked right at us, and I felt him tense up, but we were gone, me first, him right behind, holding my hand. I saw a guard with a dog just inside, and there were two with machine guns. There was a big pole to stop traffic getting through up the drive, and spikes up off the road in case anyone tried it. The road stretched off into the distance, and all the trees and grass were like a park – like paradise, like Mr Vice-President had bought up paradise and got his boys on the door in case anyone came wanting a piece of it. We ran, me laughing like we were just kids out having fun – little kids that nobody gets suspicious of – and we kept going, following the walls. We came to another gatehouse soon, just as grand, with big metal gates tight shut – and we kept on going. I guessed there'd be cameras somewhere, but the only ones I'd seen so far were at those gates, so I was more hopeful. I was pretty sure we could get into the grounds if we wanted to, just by hopping up a tree. How close we'd get to the house was another thing.

And why would our souls be singing? Maybe it was on fire, and the fat man's ass was roasting like a pig? That would be a thing to see. Anyway, that's when Raphael stopped, out of breath and sick suddenly. He pulled me back and said: 'Is this such a good idea?'

'What?' I just pretended not to understand, trying to get him on again.

'Is this a good idea? Rat, if anyone sees me . . .'

I put my arm right round him and pushed him to the side. 'Who's going to see you?' I said. 'You're asking this now? Spending my money, and all you want to do is go home?'

'I'm just thinking . . .' He was trying to be calm, but he was sweating bad. 'What are we going to find out? All we're gonna do is get ourselves chased and maybe even thrashed—'

'We've been chased before, Raphael. They don't catch us.'

'This is someone big, though. You saw the size of that dog!'

'They're for show. They're all lazy as hell—'

'We've *seen* the place,' he said. 'We can see what kind of place it is!'

I trotted on to a tree. I felt I had to keep him moving, so I pulled him towards it.

'Just follow,' I said. 'You're braver than me. We can do this!'

I got up the trunk and hauled myself higher. Raphael followed, thank goodness, and soon we were up in the leaves looking way over the fence into the promised land – I did Bible study at the Mission School and it was helping me now: I felt like little Moses. We eased out onto the thinnest, longest stem that could take our weight, and dropped easily onto the grass, rolling up onto our feet. Then we were running again, towards a little cluster of trees. Coming through them, past a little pond, we found ourselves on what I knew was a golf course, with nice little lawns and a flag, and a little sandpit for the kids. There was nobody around, but water sprinklers sprinkling, to keep the grass looking so fresh and green you wanted to roll in it. We kept low, and we tried always to be in the cover of rising ground if we could – but we saw nobody.

Soon we got to a line of huge trees, whose branches came down low. They were brushing the grass, and it was a good place to be – it was cool, and we were hidden. We were squeezing through to the other side and looking out – that's when we saw it.

Raphael said, 'Boy.'

I just looked at it, lost for words.

'How many people live there?' he said.

I laughed. I laughed for some time, and finally said, 'Do you know, I bet it's just him! I bet it's just one big man, walking around all day, looking at his money, scared to death someone's coming to get it.'

'How rich do you have to be?' said Raphael. 'Just look at it . . .'

'Look at the towers, man – it thinks it's a castle. It thinks it's in a fairy tale.'

I was drinking it in, too amazed, because I had never seen anything like it. The man had chosen his spot, I'll say that for him. He'd bought up the prettiest bit of woods in the land, and just where the grass ran down nice and flat, he'd built himself a palace, for the king he thought he was. It was all black and white wood, like stripes and crosses, with so many windows you wouldn't want to count them, let alone clean them. It was all stacked up in layers, and there was a golden dome in the middle, catching the sun – like halfway through, the builders had said they ought to try making a cathedral, just for the fun of it. At each end stood a tower with battlements, and our country's flags were waving proudly, and everywhere else were fussy little spires and statues. There was a great big fountain too, jetting up right in the front, shooting up even now, in the dry season, with nobody to look at it except us.

As we watched, coming up the drive we saw a police car. Then, just behind us – just as we drank it in and wondered – a low voice very close said: 'What are you wanting, boys?'

I cried out and swung round – but poor old Raphael was just running. He ran straight out onto the grass, then stood, not knowing what to do, like some kind of stranded cat. I held my ground and shouted: 'Stop! It's OK!' Sometimes you just know there's no danger, in a split second, and I knew the main danger was Raphael getting seen in the open.

The man's voice was calm.

The man who'd spoken wasn't angry with us. He was under a nearby tree, just back from ours, and we simply hadn't seen him – he hadn't even meant to scare us, I was sure of that. He was crouching so low and still that we'd gone right past. I could see a pair of grass-cutters in his hands, and a wide hat to keep off the sun, and it was obvious he was just a lowly old gardener, one of the hundreds they must need to keep the place so neat.

Raphael sidled back and got behind me, shaking and panting.

'You looking for anything in particular?' said the man.

'No, sir,' I said.

'Oh, just passing through. Maybe you just came to laugh?'

'What's there to laugh about?' I said.

The man smiled at us both. He could see Raph was in a state. 'I thought you must have heard, and that's why you're here. Sit a moment,' he said. 'Have a smoke. The boys at the gatehouse say we're getting a lot of people coming by, asking if the papers are true.'

'We're just roaming,' I said. 'What's in the papers?'

The man smiled again, and took off his hat. His face was so creased it looked like an old fruit – he was totally sunburned, and all I knew was, he was old as hell. A laugh came from deep down in his guts and rattled on until he was coughing, so he pulled a cigarette from somewhere and lit up, offering the pack.

'It's only been in some of the papers,' he said. 'But no one knows for sure. They don't want to admit it, that's what I think – but what are all the police cars for? That's what we're asking.'

'What *are* they for?' I said, taking a cigarette.

'You counted them? How many today?'

'Seven,' I said, shading my eyes. There were seven cars round the fountain.

'Yesterday there were twelve. Day before that . . . sixteen, and the president was here. Dropped in by helicopter.'

He started to laugh again. I passed a cigarette to Raphael, and we huddled back in the shade.

'Those police down there, fooling about. Walking in the big man's house, I don't know why. It's all over, as far as I can see – the show's over, so what's there to do? I guess they're standing around, all asking the same questions. You know who lives here, don't you? You know who you're visiting?'

'Yes,' I said. 'The senator.'

The gardener was smiling at us wider than ever, with his head on one side. 'I worked here twenty-two years,' he said. 'Spoken to him twice. First time I said, "Yes, sir," and the second time I said, "Thank you, sir." He's the fattest man I ever saw too – they had to get a car sent back and made bigger for him. I'd get sick on the food he throws away!' He coughed, and smoked deeper. 'You know, I wish I could go inside. I want to go in there and hear what they're saying. I can guess, though! It's not hard to guess maybe.'

'About what?' I said again. 'What happened there, sir?'

'He must be working hard, covering it all up, trying to save his face. He'll spend anything not to look a fool.'

I said nothing then. *Let him tell it*, I thought – *he's*

getting to it. Raphael was right behind me, listening close, and the smoke was calming him.

The old man closed his eyes and sucked on his cigarette. 'It does me good,' he said, 'just to think about it. I think all those policemen are standing around, all very polite, and saying, "Sir? Tell us again. How did you let your houseboy walk out of the door with six million dollars?"' He laughed loud and long, and Raphael started to smile too. So did I.

'Six million dollars,' the man said at last. 'Picked them up and took them out of the door. You know how he did it?'

We both shook our heads, smiling wider. It felt good just to see the old man having such a fine time, remembering it.

'Everyone here knows,' he said, 'but the papers don't have everything – they don't have the whole story yet. It was the boy they trusted.'

'What did he do?' I said. I could feel Raphael holding onto me tight, because it sounded like the pieces were fitting together. Once again, we knew we were close to whatever it was we were chasing.

'The word is, he did it with a fridge.'

'What?' I said. 'Did what with a fridge? You saying six million dollars . . . what—'

'It's what the guards say,' he said. 'One of the maids as well. The name's in the papers, but they won't say what he did. They won't say why they killed him, either.' The old man spat on the grass. 'Well – he was the houseboy here. Worked here – I don't know – not as long as me, but long. I knew him to talk to, smoke away with, and he was a nice enough boy. What I hear is that a little while back he gets told to buy a new fridge. The old one's dead, and the man needs a fridge for all that food! So – the boy orders one, and men deliver it. The boy says, "Take the old one with you, please?" Fair enough, it's got to go, it's just junk to the senator. These delivery men, they have no objections – there'll be parts they can sell. So they load it up, and our boy rides with them in the truck, with the gate pass. Chats with the guards, laughs – cool as cool. All on camera, so they say – the fridge, all roped up in sheets. But he doesn't get down. He stays on the truck to show them a short cut. Then he stays all the way. Says he wants the fridge for himself, because he knows he can make something on it. So he gives them two thousand pesos to set it down just where he wants it – and that's good money: nobody's making problems with that kind of money. Some graveyard, they say – not even a house. And that's the end of the trail. He's never seen again.'

'He'd put the money in the fridge?' I said.

The gardener was laughing again. 'That's what everybody thinks. Six million dollars in a broken fridge!'

He nodded at the house and the police cars.

'And they're just standing around, I bet. No idea

137

where it's gone. What a boy! I just wish I'd got to shake his hand.'

He stopped smiling.

'How did they get him?' I said.

'I don't know. The papers don't say.' He threw his cigarette into the grass. 'I know he had a little girl, so they could have traced her maybe.'

Raphael spoke for the first time. 'His name was José Angelico, wasn't it?' he said.

The old man looked up and stared. Then he nodded. 'You read about it, huh? You know they found the fridge? I guess they're asking where he put the cash – that's what they want. I tell you, boys, I hope he gave it away before they killed him, because I believe that son of a bitch in there's been stealing for years. Stealing even from me and you – can you believe that?'

He was shaking his head.

'Vice president,' he said, and he spat on the grass. 'I hope he never gets it back – not a cent of it. And I hope the shock kills him.'

10

Olivia's story – last section.

'José Angelico was my grandson,' said the old man.

Gardo held the cup to his mouth again. The old man drank and wiped his eyes.

He laughed briefly. 'I have many grandchildren,' he said. 'Shall I tell you why? Because Dante – you asked about him, Dante Jerome – that's my son: he adopted thirteen boys and nineteen girls.' He smiled, but it was a tired smile. 'I know that sounds impossible, but it was some government programme. You could adopt children then as easily as . . . hail a taxi. Dante started a school, you see – probably like the one you work in, Miss Olivia. And he had four children of his own, and he found that it was safest to adopt the children in his care. Every time I saw him, I'd say . . .' His voice trailed off. 'Oh my.' He scratched his head. 'Little José, little José . . . What a way to end.'

Gardo spoke again in his own language.

The old man groaned, and then he coughed and fought for breath. We waited.

'José was a favourite. One should not, I know, have favourites. But José Angelico . . . He was the sweetest boy.

He was clever too, and he did not sleep – he was always working! "I will be a doctor," he would say – so many of them say that. But . . . Oh my, we thought for a while it would come true. Olivia, is this making sense to you?'

I nodded. 'Yes,' I said. It was a lie, because I was totally confused.

'Oh, Gardo . . . you didn't bring the letter,' he said. He looked at the boy. 'Is there something in it that . . . is dangerous, perhaps?'

'We think so,' said Gardo. 'I thought the police might take it away. My friend was arrested, so we know they're looking.'

'What about his daughter? Where is Pia Dante?'

'We don't know, sir.'

'She will have nobody.' He was lost in thought for a moment, and then he said to me: 'He wrote to me every year, José. On my birthday and at Christmas. Once he wanted to be a doctor, then a lawyer. Dante would have found the money – he had ways of getting money! So many deals, the boys he put into college – if they were clever, I mean. But little José . . .' He winced and wiped his eyes. 'Not so little any more. I saw him last year – he was a man, of course. He wanted me to see his daughter – she also is my god-daughter. Oh . . .' He wiped his eyes. 'He gave up his studies years ago – he was just a houseboy, you know. Better than many jobs, I have no doubt of that, but we had hoped for better things . . . I think he lost patience.'

'Patience with what?' I said.

The old man paused. 'You cannot wait for ever. How long they keep us waiting: for ever. We knock on the door for ever? José lost patience, lost ambition, dropped out of the school. He didn't tell me where he was working. Boy,' he said, turning to Gardo. 'Please – we had better do this business. I am so tired.'

'Sir,' said Gardo.

'You asked me what *It is accomplished* meant – that was in the letter. Speak truthfully.'

'Yes,' said Gardo.

'Can you remember exactly what he said? Is this why you're here?'

'Sir,' said Gardo, 'I memorized all of the letter. If you like . . .' He looked at the door. 'I can say it to you.'

We both looked at him. 'You memorized the whole letter?' said the old man. 'By heart?'

Gardo nodded his head. 'It is not so long,' he said, smiling.

The old man sat back, and Gardo licked his lips.

'Speak.'

Gardo stood up straight. He put his hands behind his back, and I had a vision of him in a classroom, reciting.

'*To Prisoner 746229,*' he said. '*Cell Block 34K, South Wing, Colva Prison.*' He took a deep breath. '*Dear Grandfather. It is a long time since I have written to you but you have always been in my thoughts, particularly of late, and you will perhaps be happy to know that on your birthday many glasses were raised in your honour. Not a day goes by without me thinking of you, even though getting to you is so hard now, especially as duties take me away from the city.'*

Gardo paused.

'I think also of Dante Jerome, your dear son – in memoriam. I bring up my daughter to honour his memory and your own. Sir: I am to tell you something important, and it may be that I never see your face again. I tell you that the seed-corn has been planted, but not in the way you expected. Soon the harvest, I hope and pray, soon the harvest because it is accomplished, it is accomplished, it is accomplished. I say it three times, but if I could make a banner – if I could write it in the sky for you to look out on, I would do so. My friend, it is accomplished. I am writing in haste, because nothing is for certain, and I have many reasons to be cautious always, as you said to me so many times. I know they will find me. This letter will lie in a private place, with instructions. If it comes to your hand, then you know I am taken. Ask after my daughter, please – use any influence you have, for I am afraid for Pia Dante now. But the seeds are safe, sir – and the veil of the temple is rent in the midst. If only you could go to Zapanta's house now: it would make your soul sing.

'Your loving godson, José Angelico, bless you, your wife, all your many children and their memories, and all of us so lucky as to be born in your light.'

Gardo stopped, and I could see that the old man had

gone pale. His eyes were closed and he was very still. His mouth was open, and I thought for a dreadful moment that he was having a heart attack, or was about to. I could see his chest rising and falling. Gardo took up the glass of water.

'No,' said the old man. 'What he says is impossible.'

'That is the letter, sir.'

'There was something else,' whispered the man. 'He said there were instructions.'

'Sir?'

He managed to open his eyes, and all at once his face was changing colour. His face was damp again with sweat, and he turned to Gardo and reached for him. He held the boy's arm. 'Was there something else? A slip of paper?'

'Yes, sir.'

'Of course there was. There always was. Did you bring that?'

'No. I memorized . . . some of it.'

'Why only some of it?'

'Because it . . .'

'Because it was too long? Because it made no sense?'

Gardo was nodding.

'It was just numbers and slashes, wasn't it? Boy, you are chosen.'

'Yes, sir. It was just numbers, starting 940.4.18.13.14. Then I think 5.3.6.4 – I can't remember any more.'

Gardo paused, and the old man whispered, 'You

don't know what it means. You've got the instructions, Gardo – you're holding a key . . . The numbers are a code.' He spoke in his own language; he was fidgeting in his chair, trying to stand.

'You did right not to bring the letter,' he hissed. 'Oh, my boy, you are – you are an angel. You are a young, sainted angel. It's a code that we used, José and I – other boys too. It's what you call a book-code, simple when you have the book. We played games with it, but it was also for special things. Those numbers . . . they correspond to letters on certain pages – I must get my Bible. If you know where to look – if you know the rules . . . the code is so simple.' He spoke in his own tongue again. He was standing now, leaning on the table.

'What's he saying, Gardo?'

'I need my Bible. My Bible is the book we used.'

'I don't understand,' I said. The door had opened: a guard was standing there, watching us.

'Of course you don't. How could you? I'm explaining nothing, Olivia – the boy must have my Bible, and I think it will . . . oh God. I can't . . . It might reveal where the seeds have been placed. If he is serious, and he must be serious! He would not . . . trifle – he wouldn't write in that way unless it was true.' The guard walked towards us. The old man didn't notice. '*It is accomplished* was the phrase we used – it's the words of Christ, yes? – the best translation. You read your Bible? In St John, at the crucifixion: *It is finished – accomplished –* and we used it, flippantly perhaps, referring to the finding of . . . the restoration of all that had been stolen. That is what we spent our lives hoping to accomplish. Do you see now?'

A light was dawning, even on me. I said: 'Are you saying that José found some money—?'

He cut me off and turned to the guard. 'I need my Bible, sir. It's by my bed.'

The guard said, 'It is the end of the visit, sir.'

'I need my Bible, though,' he repeated.

The guard nodded, but did not move. He said something in his own language again.

The old man said, 'Please, I have to give my friends something. They have come all this way.' He spoke in his own language, and the guard looked at him steadily. When the guard spoke again, it was brief and terse.

The old man looked at me. 'He cannot help us now,' he said. 'He says that the visit is over, and nothing must leave the prison. But he says that he will help us. His name is Marco, and he says you have to go.'

'Can't we take the Bible?' I said to the guard. 'Where is it?'

'He says he will give it to you later. His name is Marco, and I have told him that it's important. He has promised. You have promised, haven't you?'

The guard nodded, and ten minutes later I was outside the prison gate, with Gardo by my side. We waited, but nobody appeared with a Bible, and the guard had gone. He had spoken in a low voice to Gardo, and Gardo had spoken earnestly back, and they had shaken hands.

'He said it is impossible to give it now,' Gardo told me as we looked for a taxi. 'But he says he will bring it to Behala.'

'When?'

'I don't know.'

'You didn't ask? What did you say to him? Is this . . . I don't understand what's going on. Will he bring it?'

'He will want money,' said Gardo softly. 'I think he will want a lot of money, but he will bring it. This is very dangerous now, for you also. He could betray us.'

* * *

The following morning, many things happened, and this is the end of my story.

Gabriel Olondriz died peacefully in the prison hospital. His death was reported in many newspapers. I assume the prison guard – the one who had the old man's Bible – realized at once that he had in his possession a precious relic of a famous old political soldier. That meant the price of the Bible could only go up. Perhaps he had overheard the old man, and understood part of the story.

Perhaps he had simply seen the light in the gentleman's eyes, and knew by instinct that there was a fortune to be made.

I never saw the guard again, because I finish here – things moved fast and I have never been so frightened.

When I got home, I went out to dinner as planned, and despite everything I'd seen, I slept well. In the early morning, however, three policemen came to my hostel, and I was asked to accompany them to a police station. My friend Mr Oliva had faxed everything to his security chief, and someone efficient put Gardo and me into some computer. I had given our Behala address, and that address must have tripped the alarm. Of course, Behala was under surveillance, and any activity from the dumpsite – anything strange – was going to ring bells and alert people.

They were there on my doorstep, three of them. I was terrified – I had no idea what to do. I got a message to Father Juilliard and he came straight away, thank God, and contacted my father. The police warned me that they would find out everything: I protected the boys as best I could, hoping to God they wouldn't be taken again. I guess I was lucky that I had understood so little. I did not mention a Bible, and I said that Gardo and the old man had spoken in their own language – that as far as I knew, they'd been talking about a house, grandson to grandfather.

Because of my father, somebody from the British Embassy arrived, and argued very strongly that I was naïve and innocent. I had also broken no law. No charges could be brought – the official kept repeating that, gently, persuasively.

After some time I was released and my passport was returned. I took advice and I was on a plane out of the country the same day.

And that is my story, and thank you for letting me tell it. I left part of my heart in your country, boys, and now I can never go back. I say to myself, so what did you learn? What did you learn from the Behala dumpsite, and how has it changed you?

I learned perhaps more than any university could ever teach me. I learned that the world revolves around money. There are values and virtues and morals; there are relationships and trust and love – and all of that is important. Money, however, is more important, and it is dripping all the time, like precious water. Some drink deep; others thirst. Without money, you shrivel and die. The absence of money is drought in which nothing can grow. Nobody knows the value of water until they've lived in a dry, dry place – like Behala. So many people, waiting for the rain.

I said goodbye to so few and I can never go back. That is a pity, and it feels so wrong, because in Gardo,

Raphael – and maybe most of all Rat – I left part of my heart, and writing this only makes me long to see you again, and this page is wet with my tears, boys.

Goodbye, and thank you so much for using me.

PART FOUR

1

This is Rat once again, aka Jun-Jun, and I tell the part where I was the leader. Where it gets bad, bloody and oh so dangerous!

It was soon after Gardo got back, with me and Raphael waiting for him by the canal, the sun going down. He got back, and the police came in. Almost before we had time to talk, we heard the siren, and oh my God, it was a river of blue! If they'd come slow and quiet, OK – maybe they'd have got us, but oh God, thank you again that they love to make a noise and have to show up like some carnival, sirens blasting out over the town. We just did the obvious thing: soon as we saw them, we made off, no time to say goodbye, just a half-minute to grab my money, and out we went. Behala's a mile wide, and there are so many ways, so I led them down to the docks, we got a garbage barge across the bay, and then walked.

Gardo has a friend of an uncle or someone who has a store selling dry goods, and we slunk in there and slept over, wondering what on earth we should do, now we were really on the run.

That's what it was for us: *on the run*, wanted men with no place to go! We had the letter still, and the map – and Gardo told us all about the Bible-code, or what he understood of it. We told him about the fridge of money and Zapanta's house, and we sat there thinking and thinking, wondering how we'd do what we needed to do – everyone sure we needed that Bible, and nobody knowing what the next step could be.

I had the idea right then, because it was clear to me we had to stay safe. I said we should lie low in one of the big tourist areas where so many street kids work and beg. There's a great gang of them there, and I'd spent some time in it after my station days. So that's what we did: we went up to the strip joints around Buendía and found a spot by a cheap hotel. We put ourselves on the edge of the crowd and tried not to draw attention. I cut off Raphael's hair, just in case anyone came looking – made him look like a little madman, though he's cute enough still – cute enough to beg from foreigners, though he wouldn't do it.

I said you got to, he said no. I said my money wouldn't last, and Gardo told me to shut up. So I sewed the cash into my shorts, and looked after us all with it, eating on the street and smoking to look rough as we could. We stuck together and stayed in the dark – stayed with the street boys for a night in the ruin of a place they used, but none of us felt safe. They weren't mean like the station boys, mainly because there's so many coming and going, but I think we were just so used to being a three. The crowd made Raphael nervous. We found a tiny room instead, high up in a stack of old shacks over a laundry. It wasn't much bigger than a coffin, but it was better than no doors, no windows, and the rent was low. We could just about sit up straight, so there we went and whispered our plans.

I made one little change, which Gardo laughed at me for – but wasn't I the hero in the end? I have never liked being nailed up inside a house, and I did it for Raphael too, who still wasn't sleeping good: I got an old tyre lever, and loosened part of the roof. Emergency exit, just in case – because we knew things were getting hotter and hotter. We knew this was real, scary heat, all around us – even in the weather there was a wind, and the freak typhoon hovering over the sea, and we all felt something big was coming. There was no way back from it now, and for the boys it meant they couldn't even see their people again – I heard them whispering and wondering, and Raphael cried at night for his auntie and his cousins.

They could never go back to the dumpsite: they had lost their homes, I guess.

We knew most of all that everything depended on that damn Bible, and the little bit of paper we had, with the lines of numbers. We had to get that Bible, and set those two things together.

So Gardo risked it, and one day borrowed my dirty clothes and walked all the way to Colva Jail.

He sat and sat, working out where the guards came

out, and he spent another two days watching the different shifts, pretending to be deaf and dumb. When he spotted the guard he was looking for, he followed him.

He followed him away from the prison, then he let the guard see him and followed some more. The guard – Marco – he just kept going and going, then found some little tea-house in the Chinese quarter. Just the two of them. That was so brave of Gardo, because we'd all worked out how the guard must know there was a price on Gardo's head. We'd gone over it and over it: the prison must have got wise to his connection to the dump, and talked to the police. They would have given anything to know what the old man and he had talked about.

The big question, therefore, was if we could trust Marco.

When Gardo came back, he told us bad news.

'The man wants twenty,' he said.

He meant twenty thousand, of course. That was the price of the Bible.

Raphael cursed and said: 'You sure he's got it? You sure he'll give it?'

Gardo thought he had, but what was dangerous was whether he'd really hand it over. He could so easily take a bit of money, say half – and then hand us in. How big a reward would they be offering for news of Gardo? The one thing none of us talked about was what would happen to us if we got arrested. We all knew that if we got taken again, we'd never get out, we'd be dead. I was getting nightmares too by this stage, waking up crying, all three of us like little boys.

But we stuck together like a gang.

'You think he'll give it?' said Raphael for the hundredth time. 'Even if we get that kind of money – you think it's safe?'

Gardo shrugged. 'We either forget it,' he said, 'and live here for ever. Or we give it a go.'

Twenty thousand pesos, though, and I had a little under two. My going-home money, squandering it on sitting around. Like I said, we all knew we were near something huge, but the thing we were near had fences all around it. Raphael read papers to me, and every day there was an update on the Zapanta robbery, with more little hints about how it happened. *Police following leads and hoping to arrest someone soon.* The fat man saying nothing, but the old scandal of what he did or didn't steal himself was being raked over again, and his big face looking dirty and not smiling any more. The stories would finish the same way every time: *Nothing ever proved against him.* Gardo told us again and again what the old man in prison had said, and we all knew who we believed.

I wanted that fat pig's money so bad I was aching, and all I could think about was fridges, and that brave houseboy on a truck, stopping at a graveyard. How he got the key and his wallet into the trash: we always wondered whether he slung it when they were chasing him, or put it there for someone special to find. We talked it through, but never found an answer – I think it must have been some last-minute desperate thing, and then they must have beaten it out of him at the police station, just before they killed him. If I get to heaven, it's the first thing I'm going to ask him. I have no doubt he's up there. None.

Anyway, to return to the story. After a week of this and getting nowhere, I decided to make my move, and get the twenty for Marco. I'd been turning it over in my head, not sharing it – but the more I thought about it, the more it seemed the only way.

I told Raphael and Gardo I was going back to Behala dumpsite, 'just to fetch something', and I thought they weren't going to let me. They said I was crazy and it was way too dangerous. They told me if anyone saw me I could be grabbed and handed over – there was bound to be a reward offered now for any one of us.

They couldn't imagine what it was I wanted to get, of course, and I didn't want to tell them for fear of bad luck. I'm just so used to keeping what I do private, I could not share what I was going to do – nor the fact I had to do it before the end of the month, which was coming up fast. All Souls' Night on its way – that's the Day of the Dead. I had to get it done before that.

I just said, 'I'm going,' again and again. Midnight came, and I slipped out through the roof while the boys were sleeping.

I did say, I think, when you look like the devil's child you can't even ride a bus.

You can hold out your money, but you still get swatted off like a fly – that time I rode with Raphael was luck, and the fact that he has a nice smile and I hid behind him. So I walked some of the way, and jumped trucks some of the way. My luck held, and got better: I found a garbage truck by the city zoo, and guess where it was going? It was going to Behala, so I got inside it. Closer to my old home, I had to be on the lookout. Other kids might jump up too, and if I was seen, the boys were right – I had no family, so I might have been sold like a dog.

We got inside the gates all right. There was a police car parked up, doors open, and that gave me a turn. But the police were just chatting to the guards, all scratching their arses, and the dogs didn't notice anything.

The truck took me past the Mission School, slowing down like it was my personal taxi. I was out fast, dropping and rolling, and I dived in under the building. The school is a big set of metal boxes, all bolted up together. The lower ones stand on legs, so there's a little bit of space beneath. I curled up here and waited for my heart to slow down. Nobody was out, it seemed, so I uncurled and moved to the back.

There's a guard at the front, but he dozes away, because who's going to break in? Who's going to steal storybooks? It would be robbing from your own people, which is why I felt so low. I was about to thieve not just from the Behala people, where I'd lived, but from Father Juilliard, who had been about the closest thing to a father I'd had so far, never knowing my real father. He was a bit slow and a bit too trusting, of course – everyone knew that. But he was a good old boy and I loved him.

I started to climb the corner.

The windows downstairs all had shutters, which were locked up at night. The upstairs windows had bars and no shutters, and I'd always made sure of an entry point. The truth was that just now and then it was nice to sleep in a big room, but I didn't make a habit of it. The other bit of truth is that I was in the bad, very bad habit of lifting money from the school safe – I did it once a month, just a little. So there were two bars I'd managed to bend so nobody would notice but my head would fit through. I was through now like a shadow, and down on the old man's bit of carpet.

How did I steal from the safe?

OK. The safe is on a table, fastened to the wall. It's not big, and it doesn't need to be because it doesn't hold much. I guess all the big money goes through banks, and they just keep a bit of cash for day-to-day stuff – a bit of cash for emergencies, I suppose – but we're still talking twenty or twenty-five thousand, so I hoped. I would never take much, just a hundred or so, hoping Father Juilliard would never miss it, and if he did, he'd think he'd miscounted. Once, twice a month at most – and that was how my little stash got to grow, which is what I didn't tell Raphael, who's more honest than me. But it's coming out now.

You're thinking, *How does a boy like a dumb rat get into a safe?* And the answer is so simple you could laugh. Father Juilliard, my friend, you must have a bad memory, because you write the lock combination in your diary. You change it every month, sir – at the end of the month – and write the new code down. I would always see it, open on your desk. I'd remember it. This month it was 20861 – I saw it when we were on the computer and you brought us that lemonade . . . but it wouldn't be the same after All Souls' Night – and that was why I'd had to make my mind up to come.

I put in that code, and the door clicked open. Inside I found twenty-three thousand and a bit more. So that was our Bible money for Mr Marco.

It went into my shorts, and I got ready to leave.

On a thought, because – please don't think the worse of me – the shame was making me ache, I stopped again. The old man's desk was full of paper, and there was a pen in the drawer. I hadn't meant to, and I knew it was a risk, but I hated the thought of you never knowing, and wondering who had so betrayed you, so I drew you a picture. I could spell Jun-Jun, so I put the words over me and a big arrow. I tried to draw me like I was hugging

Father Juilliard, who I gave a big crucifix to in case the likeness was no good. I put lots of 'x's, because I knew people used them as kisses – and I put it in the safe. I had tears in my eyes. This was a goodbye, and though Behala dump could go up in flames and I'd just dance – the Mission School had been a good, safe, warm, friendly, happy, fun place. Sister Olivia had been one of the best, and the volunteers before her. Father Juilliard had told me stories, given me food, given me money. He'd even kissed me once, which nobody before or since ever has done.

When I thought of this, climbing down the wall was hard, but I thought about Raphael and Gardo and what we had to do. I thought about José Angelico too, smashed apart by police, and I carried on.

I waited for a garbage truck to come by. I waited for it to slow. I was up on the back and inside, and we sailed out of the gates onto the street. I reached our little house well before dawn, and slunk in next to the boys so they didn't hear me. One of the nice things about Raphael is – because he slept with his little cousins, I guess – he's in the habit of sleeping up close. I crawled in under the blanket, and at once felt an arm go round me, holding me tight – and I felt less like a mean, sly, traitorous, ungrateful thief.

And he had no nightmares that night – he slept easy till sunrise, breathing soft, right on my neck.

2

Gardo again.

Rat wouldn't tell us where he got the money for two days, and when he finally did, it didn't seem like such a big deal to me, but I could see he was feeling bad so we said that if we got the Bible, and if the Bible gave away the great José Angelico mystery – and if we got to that pile of money – we would put the twenty thou back in the Mission School, with some added as a gift.

Rat was happy again, and we made some careful treks out over the city to find the guard – which we did, and we fixed up for the handover, and I knew this was the most dangerous thing yet, because he knew I was desperate for that book, which meant first it was valuable, and second – he must know something very strange was going on.

I kept thinking of being in that prison with Sister Olivia, and how they had my picture taken, and I was thinking all the time, *What if, what if, what if?* – till I couldn't sleep.

What if they stake out the tea-house?
What if they get me?
What if they just shoot me?
What if they have the whole place surrounded?

What if they're all there in plainclothes, waiting for me, and I don't see them till it's way too late?

They would break every bone in all our bodies, slow and mean and loving it.

Raphael had told me all about the window in the police room, and I knew if we were taken, none of us would come out of there. I knew I would die before I let them take me or the others: I would fight until they had to kill me, because what Raphael told me scared the life out of me, and I know I could not have done what he did.

It was Tuesday afternoon we were to meet, just after Marco's shift – same place: the tea-house in Chinatown. I washed the good clothes Sister Olivia bought me, because you don't get so many street boys round that area and I wanted to blend in more. Raphael and Rat shadowed me all the way, but separated up and keeping a distance – we didn't want to be a threesome in case policemen were waiting.

I used a fifty to buy a baseball cap, and with the trainers on I didn't look like a street boy at all, and I just walked quickly through everyone and everything – but I had my hook, though – we all did – we'd cut them down, nice and short, and mine was in my jeans at the back, where I could get it easy, and it was sharp all down the edge, because I have had to fight before, and cursed when I had nothing.

The little tea-house was dark, with shutters down, and I went straight in, not looking up, through to the table we'd used last time, right up by the kitchen, with a red lamp over it just bright enough to count out money. Marco was there before me, all alone – quite a big man, with a big, thick neck, and I slid in opposite him thinking, *Do it fast, do it fast* – I was still walking in my mind, and I wanted to be walking out of there, even though it looked like no one was around, it all looked safe, and even the kitchen was quiet.

Marco, of course – he wanted to see the money first, so I counted every note, and I could see greed in those little eyes so I thought maybe I was safe really, and twenty thousand was enough for him: I counted it out, sitting on the edge of my seat, getting ready – and he pulled the Bible out of his bag, and laid it down on the table as the Chinese who owned the place put cups down in front of us.

I told him he needed to prove it was Gabriel Olondriz' book, because I was thinking how easy it would be to give me any old Bible, then come back asking for money all over again – but he opened the cover soon as I asked, and I could see where the man had signed it, and notes – best of all, I could also see lines of letters and numbers like the code he'd talked about. Also, the whole thing was so well worn I guessed that it had to be the real one.

So I left the money where it was, took up the book, and I moved fast.

Maybe Marco hadn't expected me to just cut and run like that, but I'd been thinking how to play it, and I remembered the kitchen being near, and that was where I'd go – I jumped up and ran straight for it. Even so, I wasn't fast enough, and he got me: he kind of threw himself over the table and grabbed me hard, shouting, and the cups all crashed to the floor, and the money went everywhere, all over the floor. He half let go, panicking about the money, I think, so I got an arm free – I twisted like a fish, and saw there was someone running towards us through the shop. I heard a whistle blow then, and people were shouting – the grip on my arm got tighter, but I bucked and tore myself away, fighting for my life, I guess, and Marco was shouting: 'I've got him! I've got him!'

My hook was in my hand then.

Yes, I dragged it from my pocket, and I turned and cut up at his face: I don't know what I cut but I felt it cut through something, and the man cried out and fell backwards. He let go, of course, and I think I must have got an eye – and I'll be honest, I hope so: I hope he's a one-eyed prison guard now, and telling his tale about how he tried to sell a little boy after a deal was made, and that boy turned round and took his eye out – I hope his whole cheating face is cut right through, my gift to a filthy traitor.

I didn't have time to look, though, because I was

crashing out into that kitchen, straight into a policeman who was just running in: I went under him, and he tripped, and I slashed with my hook again but missed – and then I crashed out into a yard and over a fence, and I was running.

'Gardo! Gardo! Gardo!'

It was Rat, right on my heels: I heard two gunshots, but felt no bullets, but someone started to scream – I passed Rat the Bible and we separated, me crossing under a bridge through traffic, people watching but no one reaching for me, even when I jumped up on a taxi which was moving right at me, over the roof and rolled in the street – a moment later I was up and ducking into a fish market, and ditching my shirt – that lovely shirt – and I ran through where it was darkest, where there were boys cleaning fish over the drains, and no one was after me, but I still kept running right through and down to the canal. I swam fast to where the shacks come down to the water, and I hauled up and used my hook again to slash up my jeans and hack them short – my trainers too, I kicked them off and gave them to some kid who was watching me, and I walked along the bank, then in among the huts, praying to God that both my friends were safe, and shaking all over.

3

We were safe, but right away we knew we wouldn't be for long.

This is Raphael again, but writing it with Rat to get it just right – because the next part of this was my fault, I think. I just about saw Gardo run and Rat streak after him, and then a policeman was shouting at me, so I took off, right across the street, with the buses braking and blasting their horns. I think they must have followed me, and I'm not as quick – and even though I went the back ways, I think they saw the direction I took and made some guesses. Rat thinks maybe they photographed me and Gardo when we arrived at the tea-house.

Anyway, I think we came within an ace of being caught, and why they didn't just grab us first, I don't know. Maybe they wanted to be sure it was the Bible we wanted and needed to know why. Maybe they thought a prison guard could take on a little kid like Gardo and they'd have him for sure, cornered in a tea-house. I do not know.

Anyway, I think they must have had photographs because the next morning they were knocking on the door again, right where we lived. Rat reckons they put men out, showing our pictures and showing money, because someone gave us away . . .

4

Raphael.

We met up again early evening. We slunk in different ways, as planned, and climbed up to our little box of a house, way up the ladders to the top of the pile. We were so pleased to see each other, we just shook hands and hugged and laughed.

Rat went down to get food, as he couldn't read, and Gardo and I set to straight away, no messing. No messing.

We knew the clock was ticking, so we just drove on – you think we could have slept?

We lit a dozen candles, put them around the Bible and the paper. First we had to argue about what exactly a book-code was, and though he was the one who heard about it from the old man, I can say it was me who saw how it worked – no offence to Gardo, but I've got quicker eyes. He says we did it together, and that's true.

We sat and studied like two little schoolboys. The Bible covers were worn, the pages were dirty. Just inside the front was a column of numbers: 937, 940, 922 . . . All high numbers like that, ten of them, down in a long column. Now, we'd never been educated in numbers, but to survive you have to add up and take away – none of us were stupid, so we had some ideas.

The pages they marked were all towards the end, and Gardo remembered the old man had been talking about the Gospel.

'St John,' he said. '*It is finished.*'

That was where we started looking, and that's where a lot of fingers had been. All those pages were coloured in and used so well they were even thinner than the rest – we had to be careful they didn't come off in our hands. The bit about the crucifixion was on page 940 – the first number in the strip. So we concentrated on that page. All along the bottom, in someone's handwriting, was written:

And at that time the sky grew dark and Jesus cried out, 'It is accomplished' – and the curtain of the temple was rent in two, top to bottom – the earth quaked and the graves were opened and the saints were raised . . .

Gardo saw that each line of print had a tiny number to mark out the Bible verse, so now we tried out a hundred combinations, muddling backwards and forwards. We put the numbers in the strip against the numbers in the column. We tried counting down, and then across, but it wasn't easy because nobody knew what it was we were expecting – so he'd do one thing, I'd do another and contradict. We got to a point where we were going over the same ground again and again. All we knew was that the numbers we had – 940.4.18.13.14 – had to be set against the lines somehow, so as to turn them into letters – that was what the old man had said. But whatever we tried we ended up with gibberish.

Rat came back smelling of rum, with a nip for each of us. We ate, and he went to sleep for a while.

Gardo and me settled to trying more variations. We put out new candles, and we weren't fighting any more. He'd have a go, and hand over to me. While he tried again, I just sat and thought and thought, then he did the same.

Midnight came round, I think, and maybe that was the magic. It was the end of the month, and we were slipping into All Souls' Day – that's the Day of the Dead here. Maybe José Angelico and Gabriel Olondriz came and sat beside us – I swear it was crowded in the room. Maybe they put the answer right in his head – because Gardo hit the jackpot. Instead of going left to right, he went right to left. 4 lines down, 18 words to the left, he got a capital 'G'. 13 down, and 14 to the left, he got an 'o'. It was the first time we had a word.

He moved on 5 letters and got nowhere, so we decided that the slash might mean change the page, so we turned over. That didn't help us, so we turned the page back. 5 lines down, 3 letters in, we got 't'; then 6 down, 4 across, we got our next little 'o'. The slash meant 'turn back a page', and now we had two very meaningful words, and we just looked at them, hardly breathing:

'Go to'

We turned back a page whenever there was a slash, so we were going backwards through the book of John. It was falling out all over us, just counting carefully, straining our eyes because the words were so small. We made mistakes, but we were laughing, because the whole thing was opening up.

Go to the map ref where we lay look for the brightest light my child.

Rat woke up and we read it to him.

He shook our hands, then we hugged him, and he said: 'I know what a map ref is.' My, were his eyes big and shiny. 'I was in some class,' he said, 'and they're all doing maps. That's a map "reference", that's what it's talking about. *Where we lay* is where we were – where we met, maybe? And he's thinking his little girl is reading this.'

'Open the map,' I said. I thought even then he was being a smartarse, but we were learning to try everything anyone said, every way. 'Let's look at it again,' I said.

We'd stared at the map a hundred times, hunting it for arrows or crosses, wondering if they'd been marked and removed, straining our eyes over it. We stared and stared, and Rat said, 'A map ref is a reference to the numbers, OK? It's a line of numbers.'

'Numbers again?' I said. My head was aching, but we went back to the letter. There were no numbers apart from the code we'd just cracked, so we turned back to the map. Numbers all round the edges, but still no way in. Until I looked at the envelope and saw: *Prisoner 746229.*

I read it aloud.

'That wasn't his number,' said Gardo quietly.

'What wasn't? What are you saying?'

'When we arrived. We were in the waiting room, and the prison boss came in and asked Sister Olivia about the name. He said we had the number wrong, because at first I thought maybe we had the wrong guy completely.'

'You go up and down, that's all I remember,' said Rat – and that's what cracked it. We split the six numbers into two: 746 and 229. Sure enough, the map had a 74 and a 22, they were right there along the sides, and took us straight to a square in the middle. In it was a graveyard. In fact, the graveyard covered the square, and we never did find out what the 6 and 9 were.

'He put the fridge by a graveyard,' said Rat quietly. 'That's what the gardener said.'

'*Where we lay,*' I whispered. 'That means where we are . . . buried.'

There was a little silence, and then we all started to laugh again, quiet as we could. There was a little light coming through – we'd worked through the night, and had our answers. We held hands, we slapped our palms and Gardo kissed me right on the head. It had all just fallen all over us, and we were getting close. A graveyard in the centre of the city – the Naravo. We'd go and look for *the brightest light* – a special grave, maybe? Or a part of the church? Once again, the trash boys were ahead of the trash police.

Or so we thought.

5

This time they came quietly.

This is Jun-Jun, because I remember exactly how it was. I am the best hearer, the best jumper, the best runner – they think I brag, but they know it's true!

Early morning they came, hoping to catch us asleep – plainclothes and uniforms, I believe, all pressing in around us. The boys had blown out the candles – we were just folding up the papers, and we heard a heavy step on the ladder below.

Why I stopped and noticed, I don't know. José and Gabriel again, like Raphael says – on the Day of the Dead, the dead look after you. Anyway, I said how quiet it was – we usually heard the old lady at the bottom of the house shouting and banging about because she had about ten children, who were up before dawn making mischief. So we all stopped still, and wondered where the morning sounds had gone.

Maybe she was the one who sold us? I don't know.

I could hear someone talking below, sounding worried. Then the feet coming up the ladder sounded too heavy, that's all I can say – they sounded heavier than any man who lived up in our part of the building,

176

where you had to be light.

I went straight to the roof-hatch, opened it up.

Raphael was almost too scared to move – I had to smack him one. Gardo and he picked up what they could carry and we went so slow, so silent – because we didn't want to make a sound. If it was police, we wanted them to come right in and find an empty room. They might stick around, thinking we were close, and then bust up the next little room – the last thing we wanted was panic and for them to see us run. So even though my guts were aching and the voice inside was screaming, *Get yourself out of here!* we made ourselves go slow.

I went first and guided Raph, who guided Gardo. I was waiting for a shout, or a gunshot even – I thought they had to have the place surrounded, they wouldn't be that dumb again – but there was nobody on the roof.

Then, just below, I heard someone call Gardo's name.

'Hey, Gardo! It's your cousin!'

Lies.

'Gardo? Hey! He's sick.'

Crazy lies, telling us only that we had to get moving.

We stayed low, poised there for a while, like three scared little cats. I beckoned, and we all crossed to the next roof, a TV aerial helping us swing down silently. There were wires stretching across, but we all knew not to touch them in case they were bad electrics – once you've had a zap off a power line you go careful. So we just went on our toes down into a dip in the roof-space where we definitely couldn't be seen.

Luck holding.

A man was sitting in his window, smoking a cigarette, just watching us. I saw some other people too – a woman flapping out some washing, and two children playing with a dog. Everyone stopped and stared at us, but no one said a word and the dog didn't bark.

Then down below we heard battering and hammering on doors, and we knew the police were moving. Right at once we heard feet running, we heard shouting – we could hear big dogs, and engines were revving. All of a sudden, over a ledge and level with us, there was a policeman coming up a ladder – and he was looking right at me.

He shouted something, and got a whistle in his mouth. Then I saw him go for his gun, but he was clinging to the ladder still, and we were gone before he could aim. Under us and all around us, though, the world was full of noise.

6

Raphael.

Running for your life two times in one day? We were so scared, both times, we thought our hearts would just blow apart. But the thing is, when we thought about it later, Rat had been chased so often, and grabbed at so often, that he must have had extra senses. When he was on the station, it was bad, but it could be bad at Behala too – someone thinks it's fun to grab the skinny kid with the crazy teeth and see what he's got. When Rat sees someone move, his feet get ready to jump.

The policeman with the gun was slow, but what was so dangerous was how many more there might be and how quick we had to be. Rat led, and got to the edge of our roof, and over a low wall. From that we hopped down onto a long warehouse roof, and we ran right along its guttering. We were clear for a moment, but then we saw a policeman in the grass below, bursting through a gate – and it's the same thing again: his gun's out and he's got a whistle to his lips. He had no chance to fire because we got straight round some chimneys and then up the slope – but he'd have a radio, and soon they'd be all around us, we all knew that. We had to think so quick – and let's just thank Rat again for being the one who'd got to know the area. He was the one who spent the time checking in with the street kids, so he was the one who saw the chance and went for it.

The next-door building was the very one where those children lived, where we'd all spent the one night. Rat saw at once we had to dive back in among them. How were the police going to take in a hundred kids? It was the smartest thing he ever did.

Now, the place they lived – the place we were opposite now – was a big old block of flats that had caught fire years ago – just a big, black, ugly cement thing, nobody knowing what to do with it. The gang lived there – a hundred or more, scavenging, begging, sweeping and doing things you don't want to know about. They'd get cleared out, and come back again, then a big clearout, and back they come – that's how it always was in these old places.

The roof we were on ran right up to it, and one jump would get us in the window. As we got to the edge, we could see some of the kids sorting out their breakfasts. A little one looked right up and waved.

It was a long jump to get to it, and I know Gardo and I just looked for a moment, too scared to try. But we did it, Rat first, and Gardo next, and me . . . I just threw myself, and they caught me somehow, dragged me up so I was bloody again. We ran then, through the kids that had come to see us, to help us, and they clustered around – they knew we were running because there's not many kids that haven't had to do the same thing – and they were wild for us. We all ran together. We found stairs down, and everyone was screaming and laughing, shouting to their friends, so suddenly we were a mighty crowd, pouring into the hallway.

It saved us, I swear.

When we reached the street, we just streamed out, wild as birds, screaming over the street in all directions. There were two police cars, another one roaring in. There were men with radios, guns out and arms wide to catch us, staring around wildly as this mass of little boys and girls rolled out over them. One grabbed a kid, and everyone flew away from him, howling out and laughing like it was a game, straight into the street, where a truck had to slam on its brakes and a bus swerved round up over the kerb, straight into the police car.

Then, just like birds, we were all gone, spreading out and ducking through the alleys and store-fronts, policemen running but hopeless. It was all three of us and about five or six other boys, but then they flew off on their own, and the three of us were safe, still running till we reached a road.

Then, an amazing thing.

Gardo did something so smart I think Rat kissed him, but he says he didn't! Cool as anything, he held up the money we had left to a slow-moving taxi cab. I think the driver was so stunned he just pulled over, and we piled in before he could smell us. A few minutes later we were off again, on the South Superhighway, and he had twice the fare in his hand and he was smiling too.

'Where you going?' he kept saying. 'Where you going?'

'Naravo Cemetery,' we said.

Where else would we go? The square on the map.

And on this particular day, you know – another funny thing – probably half the city was heading that way too – we were just running with the flow. The Day of the Dead, and the Naravo's the biggest graveyard in our city: everyone goes there, rich and poor alike. So we got down low in our seats, and soon our happy driver was up the ramp and driving fast, overtaking buses and trucks. He put his radio on, and we sang.

We wound down the windows and we sang louder as the sun came up higher, right in our eyes. OK, it wasn't over, not at all. But we were alive another day, and that was worth singing for!

7

My name is Frederico Gonz, and I make grave memorials.

One small detail from me, for Father Juilliard. You ask, sir, so I will tell you.

I met José Angelico the way I meet many of my customers. I have a workshop on the cemetery road, just past the coffin makers. I specialize in the small, simple stone. I am very aware that my clients have next to nothing, and renting the grave has often taken most of their money. So I modify and modify and get down to the very lowest cost. The dead, however, must have that stone: the reminder, the eternal reminder, that this man, this woman, this child – existed.

On some of the graves the name is marked in paint, or even pen, and everyone knows how sad that is. Make something out of stone, I say, and no one touches the grave. The poor are not buried, you see. There is not enough ground here any more, so in the Naravo they build upwards. The graves of the poor are concrete boxes, each just big enough for the coffin. They go up and up – in some parts twenty boxes high. A funeral here is to slide the coffin in and watch the sealing of the compartment. Part of my service is that I cement the stone that I've made into place, and thus seal the chamber.

José Angelico used me when his son died. I was sad to see him again with news that his daughter had died also. It meant he had no one in the world now.

He was a thin, lean, gentle man who always spoke quietly. I knew that he was a houseboy for a rich man, but that was all I knew. He found me early in the morning, and he looked as if he hadn't slept for a long, long time. He gave me just a morning to make the stone, which is unusual, but he said he had run out of money for the funeral home, and the coffin had to be moved that day. It would be a simple ceremony, he said, because there were no relatives.

I offered him all my sympathies, and he paid me two hundred as a deposit, and I set to work.

Pia Dante Angelico: seeds to harvest, my child were the words he chose. *It is accomplished*.

I did not chisel it myself. My son is ten years old, and is a fine cutter now. He used to rough out and I would finish. Now, he finishes, and he's developing his own style of turning letters – small flourishes that add elegance to elegant words. He completed the stone in four hours, and we set it by for pick-up.

How was I to know it was lies? He looked to me so meek and so mild – there wasn't a lie in his face. He took the stone and paid me from a small leather bag. He had the coffin behind him, carried by two young men – street sweepers, they looked like. No priest. I went along and saw the coffin placed inside, and we said prayers for the child. I sealed it and fixed our little stone. All I could see was the worry and grief, like he was a man worn down to nothing. There wasn't a lie in his face.

When I read about him dying in a police station, I just thought, *Poor man*. I read the story to my son, and we said a prayer for him also.

STAR EXTRA:
Police Closing in

A spokesman for the city police said last night that important leads are being followed up 'professionally, vigorously and relentlessly', and that the undisclosed sum stolen from the vice-president's house would undoubtedly be recovered. 'You cannot keep this kind of money hidden. Experience tells us that somebody, somewhere, will blow the whistle soon. That is when we swoop.'

Requests for further details were firmly declined. 'We are at a sensitive stage. We are talking to people who have to stay anonymous. All we can say is that we are confident that a breakthrough is imminent.'

Vice-President Zapanta is no stranger to controversy and has been constantly dogged by accusations and scandal. Trained as a lawyer, he has been notoriously quick to challenge and in many cases prosecute critics of his policies and personal conduct – to date, successfully. A spokesman for the senator reported that he was in 'considerable distress but remains hopeful'.

Sources suggest the criminal was a member of the senator's domestic staff. The president herself, who visited Zapanta last Thursday, said, 'Our thoughts are with any colleague who experiences loss. Theft is theft: one feels violated, always.'

Vice-President Zapanta remains a key witness in the ongoing prosecution of his subsidiary company, Feed Us!, which collapsed with debts of two million dollars and was subsequently implicated in the hiking of rice import duties during the economic downturn last year.

The trial is now in its fourth year and the *Star* wishes to reaffirm that the vice-president denies all charges.

INQUIRER:

Zapanta mourns his loss!

Vice-President Senator 'We are the people' Regis Zapanta is said to be 'extremely concerned' at the loss – that is, the theft – of an undisclosed sum of money from his property last week. Sources close to the great man say that you can hear a pin drop – a banknote fall – and even the occasional groan of despair. Sources even closer say our much-loved vice-president is 'enraged' – and we all know what the senator's rage has accomplished in the past.

Senator Zapanta achieved notoriety just three years ago when he ordered police to clear squatter camps to make way for his ground-breaking cinema/shopping complex. He was also made famous by a dramatic poster campaign aimed at the illiterate, featuring laughing orphans holding placards that spelled out his name – the children received no fee for their services.

The vice-president has always campaigned for wider education, whilst presiding over an education budget that has dwindled by 18% over two years.

He was not available for comment.

"WHAT THE HELL ..?"

187

Mohun's diary

Check out the face of super-smiling Regis Zapanta, who's now wearing a frown – just as the wind appears to be changing! Could the rumours be true? Is our man, who's spent a lifetime swearing he's clean, as oily as a back-axle?

If he really has lost ten million dollars, someone's going to ask the question: 'What was ten million dollars doing in your house, sir?' We all need ready cash. We all keep a stash of change . . . But ten mill in dollars, just in case the ATMs are down?

Ten mill under the bed suggests someone's either not paying their taxes, or stealing other people's.

I didn't say that, sir – don't close my paper, don't shoot my family!

Enough is
enough, say students

THE VERY FACT THAT
VICE-PRESIDENT Senator
Regis Zapanta keeps millions of
dollars of cash in his home
suggests that he is part of a
corrupt other world – and
should not be re-elected. This
country could still move forward, but it won't until we've
said goodbye to bad, greedy old
men.

It's time for someone young
and new!

Charuvi Adarme, president
of the students' union, made
her feelings plain in an im-
passioned address yesterday to
those on the diploma
programme.

'Five years ago,' she said,
'Zapanta campaigned on the
slogan, *The brightest smile, the
sharpest mind.* I'd add to that,
*The most questionable conscience
and the blackest heart.* He's
spent more than three decades
lining his pockets, and his main
achievement is that he's made
the country's poor feel worth-
less and powerless.'

What does the country need
right now?

THREE THINGS:

A revolution.

Then a revolution.

Then – when the dust has
settled – a revolution.

PART FIVE

PART FIVE

1

Raphael, Gardo and Jun-Jun (Rat):

The Day of the Dead is about the biggest festival of the year out here – bigger even than Christmas and Easter together. It's when ten million candles get lit, and the ghosts come up and walk around arm-in-arm, and everyone goes to see their departed ones, who stand up out of the ground and say hello.

That was why the traffic soon got slow, and before too long we were in a long jam – at last the taxi dropped us on the road that led off to the cemetery, and we walked in the smell of flowers.

There were crowds pushing everywhere.

People walked with kids and babies in their arms, whole big families, and some of the men had tables on their heads and chairs in stacks, on trolleys; they had cases of beer, great big bottles of water, and the ice carriers were dragging great slabs of ice, shouting for a way through. Little stoves, bags of food, and people dressed up as best they could, as if for a carnival – little girls in new dresses and the boys in ties, even though it was a hot morning. This is the day when your family is together again. You set up house by the grave, and sit and chat and eat and drink right on to midnight. By the time it gets to evening, the whole cemetery is glittering with the candles – and that's when they say you need an extra chair, and an extra glass. That's when you can turn round, and dead Grandma's right beside you, old bones in whatever you buried her, smiling away with a hundred stories to tell. That's when the kid you lost is playing around at your feet again, and if you had some quarrel with a brother who died, you can talk it through and settle it. Father Juilliard told Rat all about the resurrection one time, and I guess it's this that he was talking about.

Rat says: I've never seen it, of course, but then I have no family here. I do believe in ghosts, though, and on Sampalo island, where I'm from, people say they come out of the sea sometimes, if a boat goes down. They come into the village, sad as sad, and cry by your door all night. What do I know, though? I'd seen nothing like this.

Around us, the flower shacks got thicker and were overflowing with flowers till the scent lifted you off your feet. There were stores with sweet little Bible verses, plastic statues, plaques and postcards. The lottery sellers were everywhere, carrying wads of tickets and shouting. After all that, we came to the candle stalls – so many candles, thick and thin, tiny as your finger or too big to carry. Back from them there were food stalls, doing good business – and the three of us stopped and ate some fish, because we were hungry again and hadn't had breakfast.

* * *

Raphael: I cleaned the blood off my arms, and Gardo said it was time for a plan. Opening up the Bible, we sat eating and reading, and nobody bothered us, because who's going to get upset about even street kids, if they're reading the Bible on All Souls' Day? There was that breeze again, getting stronger still with all that flower smell, and we could feel the freak typhoon coming in on us again, ripping at the tents. It was going to be hard keeping the candles lit, so there were lots of people buying little jars for that reason.

I said, '*Where we lay*,' and I scratched my head. 'I guess he's buried here. Does that make sense?'

'He won't be buried anywhere,' I said (this is Gardo). 'If the police killed him, he's going to be burned up by now and in the trash. Also, he must have wrote all that before he died.'

That was true and we all agreed. But we also thought, *What if his wife's buried here?* If that was the case, then *Where we lay* could mean the family grave. And that was what we decided to look for.

Rat now: I felt bad then, because that meant reading was needed. I couldn't read, and that meant I'd be no use.

195

There was nothing for it, though, so we finished our fish and started, and I carried the papers and the book and followed on.

Like I said, it's the biggest graveyard in the city. Once through the gates, there were walkways spreading off to left and right, stretching for miles. We were soon lost in graves, trees and monuments. There were bushes and shrubs, and as we walked, great big angels would suddenly appear at you out of the leaves. Peaceful-looking Madonnas looking into the distance, and weepy little Jesuses on tiny little crosses, and then big-brother Jesuses stretched out, with eyes up to heaven. I had never been watched over by so many saints and I nearly got split up from the boys looking at them.

The tables were going up and picnics were opening. The parties were starting, and soon Raph and Gardo knew they'd never find one name in all these millions.

'We can ask,' said Raphael. 'There's an office with lists of names . . . is that a big risk?'

'Everything is,' said Gardo, looking around, still looking mean. 'Everything has been.'

That was when I said I would do it. I said, 'I can pretend Mrs Angelico did me a good turn and that I've come to say hi.'

So Gardo counted me back a bit of my money – he'd become the money-man after the deal with Marco. 'Get her some flowers,' he said. 'That'll make it real.'

That's what I did, and it took three hours or more. There was a big queue of people, and I kept getting shoved back. When I got a guard to see me, he said he needed twenty to check the record – which was a lie, but I gave it to him. Then he went off and took ages, answering all sorts of other questions from people, so I just sat with my flowers, hoping he wouldn't forget me altogether. It was late afternoon when I got my slip of paper, and Gardo thought I'd been off drinking.

'B twenty-four/eight,' I said to Raph. 'He says, "Top of the slope and look for a pink angel."'

'It's getting dark,' said Gardo. 'Can you see pink in the dark?'

Raphael led the way, strong again, and ready.

Raphael now.

It was getting busier and busier because the evening is the busiest part of the day. There were barbecues starting up now, and people selling snacks. We were amongst wealthy people in very fancy clothes, and we felt even greyer and dirtier, but there was nothing for it, and still nobody was worrying about us – no one seemed to see us, like we were the ghosts.

After twenty minutes we got to the top of the slope.

I saw so many angels, and the light was way too bad to see a pink one, and I was ready to curse the guard who wasted our time – but then Gardo saw one made of marble, on a grave the size of a truck. In the candles it was pink as a salmon, and it was staring back over the city, arms up like it had just scored one hell of a goal. A great big family were sitting all around it, playing cards, and there were brandy bottles everywhere, and more people arriving, hugging each other.

We left them to it, and went in and out of the neighbouring graves, wondering what B24/8 might mean, and looking for the name 'Angelico', and finding nothing.

Soon it was completely dark, and we couldn't read the names any more. So we went back to the pink angel, and climbed up on a wall nearby, and wondered what to do.

And that is when we saw *the brightest light*.

2

Raphael, Gardo and Jun-Jun (Rat):

We'd been looking in the wrong place, and the fool of a guard who took our money must have thought we knew the cemetery and didn't bother to explain, or was just too lazy. The cemetery, you see, is divided by a wall – and that was the wall we were sitting on. The wall divides the rich quarter, where the dead get buried in earth, from the poor quarter, where the dead get stacked up in boxes.

We'd wasted the day walking among the rich when we should have been on the other side of the wall. The brightest of lights was the poor part of the cemetery, where thousands of candles were coming together as everyone streamed in after work. It was bright as day, bright as a furnace, and the candles were moving in great rivers as people made their way to their loved ones. It was like a little town down there, with narrow streets through all the tombs.

B24/8 would be the number of one of the concrete boxes.

Raphael: I remember Gardo looking at me and smiling, and then Rat gave me a hug because we'd cracked it again.

We jumped down and came to a little broken doorway that let you into the other side. Right away, we saw a sign in the candlelight, high up on one of the grave-stacks. It said G9, so we moved past it, trying to work out the system.

It really was like a town: people lived in this part of the cemetery – they had houses there. There were little shanties built round the back of the grave-boxes. There were shacks up on top too – little huts and bits of plastic, and to get to them you climbed ladders. We could see kids running on the tops with a kite, getting it up into the typhoon breeze. So many people always, and it struck me again what my auntie used to say: there is nowhere people will not live.

We passed so many graves.

Saddest were the open ones – the ones that were broken open – and everyone knows that story, and I found myself looking away. Each little concrete hole costs the family two thousand-five for five years. You cannot buy a box, you see – you can only rent one. After five years you pay again, or the box is taken back. And people move away, or people spend the money, and sometimes the payment just doesn't get made – so what happens? The sledgehammer is what happens. They break open the seal, and out comes the body. There's a part of the cemetery where old bones are thrown and left to rot amongst the trash. Somebody's child, or somebody's grandma – out on the rubbish like a dog. The empty holes scared me, because nothing is more sad than that, and I didn't want to look. They leave the bodies in there for a few weeks sometimes, hoping they'll be claimed, because I guess nobody likes throwing people away like that.

* * *

Gardo.

I was working it out though.

I led them round the back, and talked to some kids perched up on the grave-stacks. They pointed, and we found the track that was D, then C, then B, so then we came along, counting – fifteen, twenty and twenty-two. Four graves up, and there she was, we found her: *Maria Angelico, wife of José Angelico*, picked out on a little stone plaque. Raphael and me climbed up and leaned in to read, because the words under the name were small. *The brightest of lights*, they said, and I went cold, because those words were the ones we'd been following, and what we'd seen, and it was all coming together – we were close to the end. Around the words were scorch marks, from the candles that had been lit. Raphael read the words out to Rat, calling out loud because there were people everywhere and a lot of drinking going on and a lot of laughter. I looked at the box underneath, and I called that out too:

'*Eladio "Joe" Angelico*,' I said. '*My good, good son.*'

Raphael grabbed me and said, 'We're where we're supposed to be! This is his boy.'

201

I said, 'I know that.' That was clear. But I was also thinking . . . *What's there to find? We've found the poor man's family grave – is that really such a big deal now? This sad man, whose face we first saw when we found a wallet on the dumpsite . . . he loses his wife and his boy and we're poking around, hunting his money? He couldn't have hidden it here.*

'We're where we should be,' I said. 'But he can't have put it in a grave.'

'I agree, ' said Rat. 'How would he do it?'

'What's that one there?' said Raphael, looking up. 'Is that his as well?'

He was looking at the stone above the man's wife, and I had to climb higher up to see that one. It was clean and new, and the words were harder to read because the light was bad, so Rat handed me up a candle, and I figured them out slowly, Raphael helping.

'*Seeds*,' I said. 'Something about those seeds again . . . Then it says: *To har . . . vest. My. Child. It. Is* . . . Something long, I can't see.'

'Accomplished,' we said, together.

'*It is accomplished*,' I said. '*It is accomplished. Love and . . . hope.* And there's a name – just a little name,' and I traced it with my finger.

Raphael.

The name on the stone was *Pia*. Then, *Dante. Pia Dante.*

I looked down at Rat. 'Oh my,' I said, and I felt so sad. 'That's the little girl.'

I thought of the photo, of the little schoolgirl with her wondering eyes, and felt so bad. We'd all thought she was alive, or hoped she was.

Rat said, 'He lost everything, man . . .'

'He was sending her to school,' I said. 'That's what the paper said.'

'It was in the letter too,' said Gardo. 'The letter to Mr Olondriz. *If it comes to your hand, then you know I am taken. Ask after my daughter, please – use any influence you have, for I am afraid for Pia Dante now.*'

We were quiet a moment, and then I jumped down.

'What now?' I said. 'What are we expecting to find here? What do we do?'

Gardo said, 'I don't know.'

I said, 'A message, maybe? Look for another message . . .'

'Where?' said Rat. 'Where's he going to put it?'

We all looked around wildly, maybe thinking there'd be a letter, or some other clue – but it seemed pretty hopeless – it all seemed like a dead end.

'We've got this far,' said Gardo, getting angry like he does. 'There must be something!'

'Nothing,' said Rat. 'Where's there to look, and what are we looking for? I think he was taken and killed before he could do anything.'

'Maybe the police have been and got it?' I said. 'They tracked it other ways maybe.'

Gardo sat down again. 'Why is this so crazy?' he said.

I sat next to him, and we thought and thought, but there was nothing to think. Then, right by us, a big family arrived, pressing into the graves with a load of candles and a cooking stove, so we moved off across the path and found a quieter place, higher up.

'Look,' I said. I couldn't let it go. 'If he had all that money . . . If he got away with it – if he really had a fridge full of money . . . Are we thinking he buried it here, with his wife and kids? Why would he do that?'

'To come back later and get it,' said Rat. 'No one's going to break open a paid-for grave, are they?'

'The police would,' said Gardo. 'If they had even one slight suspicion. That's why the code. If the police had got the letter we got – if they did what we did – went to the prison and saw Mr Gabriel . . . he would not have let on about the Bible and the book-code. So they would never have got this far.' He smiled, and said what we all knew: 'The man was smart.'

'OK,' said Rat. 'So José Angelico knew he could trust Gabriel Olondriz. Gabriel was like the . . . guardian of it. Without him it's never found. If it's in there, even.'

'You think it's in there?' I said.

'It's in one of them,' said Gardo. 'Maybe.'

'You want to break open three graves?' I said. I

couldn't believe I was even thinking about it. I knew I couldn't do it.

Gardo stood up then. He walked up and down, and I could see him thinking so hard his eyes were bulging, getting madder and madder. 'It can't be!' he said. 'You don't do that, do you? You don't bust open your family grave! What about an empty one? Maybe there's a broken one nearby . . .'

We looked around, and there were several. You could see what looked like trash, or maybe bones. Who wanted to sort through that? One thing for sure was they weren't places you'd leave anything valuable. Gardo was beginning to really lose his cool, and I could see why – we'd come all this way, and had the police all over us – he'd been almost taken, fought his way out . . . and all for nothing? He looked at me and said, 'What do we do, Raphael?' and I didn't know. I just looked at him, and Rat was looking from him to me then back again.

It was just at that moment, as we were gazing around, that we heard a voice.

It was a small voice, and it was calling down to us, and was almost blown away by the wind. But we just caught the sound, and looked up to see a tiny little girl.

'What are you looking for?' she said.

3

Raphael, Gardo and Jun-Jun (Rat):

She was sitting up on the graves, higher than us, so she was looking down. She was hard to see, because like I said she was so small, and there weren't so many candles there. She had long black hair, and was sitting patiently, her hands in her lap. She was wearing school dress.

Rat said, 'What did you say?'

The little girl said, 'Who are you looking for?'

Raphael said: 'José Angelico.'

'I don't think he's coming,' said the child.

We didn't know what to say for a moment, and then Gardo said: 'Did he say he would? When?'

We were all staring up at her and she was just staring down, so still. The breeze blew her hair, but she was like a little statue.

'About a week ago,' she said quietly. 'I've been waiting.'

Gardo said, 'I don't think he's coming either – why don't you come down here?'

'What's your name?' said Rat softly. 'What are you looking for?'

'I'm not looking for anything,' she said. 'I just came here to wait for him.'

'But where do you live?'

'Here. I don't know now.'

'By yourself? What's your name, *chele*?'

'Pia Dante,' she said. 'My name is Pia Dante Angelico and I'm waiting for my father, José Angelico.'

Now, I (Raphael) speak only for myself and not for the other boys, but I went stone-cold all over and I nearly fell down. I heard Rat breathe in sharply too and take a pace back. Her hair was still blowing and she looked solid enough, and her voice was a child's voice . . . but my first thought was that we must be talking to a ghost, because we'd seen her grave with our own eyes.

The child was looking across at it – B25/8 – the grave with her own name on, in brand-new stone. And she was waiting for her dead father on the Day of the Dead. What kind of miracle was that?

4

Raphael, Gardo and Jun-Jun (Rat):

She was no ghost, of course, and when we got ourselves together, we helped her climb down. Rat went up and helped her, because she was small – and we decided to take her out of there fast. Things were getting so strange, and we were all having the same idea straight away, but we needed to get clear for a while. Little Pia was so weak she could hardly stand up, and we all realized none of us had eaten properly, and we thought, *We've come this far – the police aren't going to trace us here – can we just get a moment to think?*

Gardo counted out the money, and we were low – our stash was down to a few hundred only, but we all needed food – little Pia most of all. I tell you, she was skin and bone to touch, and dirty all over – she smelled bad. We went right out of the cemetery and found a shack and ate chicken and rice, thinking we might as well eat good – we so needed it. We were at the end of the trail, we had to be, and even at that point – before we talked – we knew what was happening, and we were getting excited, frightened, jittery. Cold and sweating – like a fever.

Rat and Pia were just about the same size, and he

could see she was in a bad way more than me and Gardo. He's been starved like that and scared out of his wits, so he knew what to do. He made her eat really slow, mixing gravy into the rice and feeding her. He got her water and made her drink it, and then he found her some banana, which he chopped up small like she was a baby. In a way she was a baby. She was scared, but she was so weak she didn't know what to do, and we still think Rat saved her life.

She told us she'd been in Naravo for a week, to meet her father. It was a place they often went together, because her little brother and her mother were there.

Some children had found her and taken her to one of the shanties – she'd been fed a bit and asked questions. She kept going back to her mother's grave and waiting, and of course she wasn't tall enough to read her own name on the grave above – or if she did, it didn't mean anything to her – she never said anything about it. Her father had sent her a message to meet him, and whoever looked after her had taken her there and left her. They must have read about his death, and knew they were well rid of her, what with no more rent coming in.

Pia Dante was alone.

Gardo: We talked to a boy at the eating house, and for fifty got her space out the back for the night, and Rat laid her down, and got an extra blanket because a typhoon wind is cold for a child. I saw him smoothing out her hair, wrapping her up, talking to her and promising we'd be back to look after her. Then he came over to me and Raphael – he was crying. I'm putting that in because I think it's important – it's the only time we ever saw Rat cry.

All of us knew now that this was the time to thrash it all out and do the final, final plan. We ordered tea, and I – Gardo – spent seventy on a bottle of brandy, and I made us all take three fingers, because what lay ahead was the hardest, and yet in a way it was also just free-fall now, the plan so clear we couldn't go outside it. Three fingers was enough, because we needed to be brave for the next bit – braver even than my friend and brother Raphael in the police station, because nobody goes among the graves on All Souls' Night after midnight, because that is when the dead are left to themselves again, so the ghosts are getting sad. We knew we had to, however – there was no question – because it was the only time we could do what we had to do. Can you blame us if we stoked up on drink?

'We need tools,' I said, and we worked out what we needed.

'We're going to need a way out too,' said Raphael, and we planned out our route.

I said, 'What does six million dollars look like?' I think the brandy was hitting me and making me smile. All of us then, we started to laugh – for the first time in what seemed a while. And do you know what, we knew it wasn't ours, even then – and couldn't be ours. We knew that a piece of it was all we wanted, and we knew we were so close, the air was buzzing around us, as if the ghosts were above us! That much money, if it really was there – six million. I promise you, the one thing we all knew was that it was not ours and we would not even try to take more than a little.

We split up to look for tools, saying we'd meet at the grave as soon as we could. We knew it without saying it: we had to go back and smash in the slab and get inside. I am sure we agreed that, without quite saying it. Raphael went off and found a sack and a cheap old broken knife. I went scavenging close up under the shanties where the graveyard turns to swamp and sea: I found a strong iron spike. It was tying up someone's boat, so I tied it to a wooden stake, and took the spike, quiet as the breeze. Rat found rope and a plastic sheet, which was everything we needed.

I'd said to Raphael, 'We do this job fast – once we start, we do not stop,' and we hugged each other.

I'm Raphael. I said to Gardo, 'It's going to make a noise. We do it fast, OK?' We finished the brandy and felt stronger and better.

Gardo again.

We climbed up to little Pia's grave-box. I think there

were ghosts everywhere, just watching. Raphael held the spike and Rat passed up a stone.

Everyone had gone, and most of the candles had blown out, because the typhoon was getting closer and the wind was strong and cold, nagging at us – I didn't have a shirt and I could feel it, right in off the sea. I swear I could feel them all, those dead, around me still, watching me with wide-awake eyes. Dead men above and below, and dead kids and dead mothers – I could almost see them, watching and watching, and I so didn't want to look up.

The stone was good in my hand, just the right size. Raphael had the spike in the corner, and I leaned back and gave it the most almighty crack. The thing moved right off, and the noise was more of a thud – a real, deep, dead sound. I guess because the seal was so new, it hadn't got itself all fixed and hard, but the second blow punched it right in, and it fell on itself in three big pieces, one of them falling nearly on Rat's feet, so he jumped back. Then he was up with rope and candles, right up against me, and we were lighting them fast inside the grave-hole where the wind couldn't get.

The air was musty, but there was no bad smell. There was a coffin, white as white – for a child – and we all felt scared, I guess. It had a layer of dust, and the flowers on it were very dead – other than that, everything was fresh. No smell – and we all knew what dead things smell like, because people throw dead things out on the dumpsite. I found a dead kid once, and there's no mistaking that particular stink, once you've had it in your face.

We threw out the other bits of broken stone and eased her out.

Back to me, Raphael. Like Gardo says, the wind was getting up and it made us want to work faster than ever. Rat got the rope around the coffin. Then, as we slid her out, he squeezed right into the hole so he was safe and firm. That meant he could let it down to us, because six million dollars in a wooden box . . . I tell you, six million dollars in a box is heavy, if that's what was in the box – don't forget we didn't know that for sure. We only thought we knew, but it felt as heavy as that kind of money ought to be. We got her on the ground, and though we'd all said we'd move fast, we had to see what it was inside, right there and then.

The knife was our screwdriver. Eight screws held the lid, and I know, lifting a coffin lid . . . you think of all the evil things in the world – in a graveyard, in the middle of the night – but I think all three of us knew in our hearts now, so we just did those screws and lifted it, and like Gardo says, the ghosts were around us, watching.

Oh sweet Lord, the money was there.

The money was there. It was packed in so snug it was like the box was made for it.

You want to know what six million looks like? I will try to tell you.

To me, sitting next to it, it looked like food and drink, and changing my life – and getting a way out of the city for ever. It looked like change, it looked like the future. I don't know what it looked like. We stared a moment, and nobody spoke. We had the plan, and the plan was not finished yet, and none of us suddenly thought, *Let's keep it all* – nobody even suggested we change the last part of our plan. We knew the money wasn't ours, because even though I never met that man, Gabriel Olondriz – the way Gardo had told us about him, I knew he was a good man, through and through. It was All Souls' Night, and he was there, I hope and believe, at the front of the ghost-crowd! Right there with us. I think he stayed with us too – I hope with José Angelico, arm in arm – with us all the way.

5

Jun – no longer Rat. My name is Jun-Jun.

And the boys have given me the last part of the story – I guess because the last part was my idea. They dispute that – Gardo says it was his, because he was the only one of us who met Mr Gabriel, but I was the one who knew how to do it – and it did get done at what was once my home, or just above it.

Also, Raphael – he had the whole first part of the story, and I think he knows we tell it together, better, because we are a team now. Who cares, in the end? Who cares who did what when the whole point was we did it together?

We'd talked it all out, asking the same questions: what do you do with six million dollars? How are you going to spend it? Or what would we do, the three of us? Line up in the bank the next morning and ask to put it in a safe? Bury it some place else?

The one thing we knew is that as soon as we had it, it would be taken away – you think we stood a chance of keeping even a million? So I said we should take it to Behala and put it in the trash for anyone who finds it.

Maybe it was the brandy, but what I remember is the boys just laughing at me, and laughing at each other.

We shook it all out of the coffin into the sack and the sheet. José Angelico's money: the money stolen by the senator-vice-president from hell, from all his own people. We roped up the sack and the sheet and got them on our backs. We took them over the wall, just in case the gates were guarded – every gate in this city is . . . We stopped off for Pia, of course, and she was so sleepy I had to carry her on my back, so Gardo took one sack, Raphael the other – and off we went into the wind, which was getting strong now, racing along the streets and making a noise, rolling trash ahead of it.

Who did we meet? Who else could we meet but a little gang of baby trash boys doing the night shift, scavenging about with a cart. Gardo showed them a note, and it was like a charm. Half a minute and our bags were in the cart, and Pia was on the crossbar, and we were pedalling through the streets, all of us clinging on and singing out. Who's going to stop a crowd of filthy trash kids fooling in the night? We passed a police car sitting by a junction, and we even waved. It was the early hours of the morning and the wind was behind us all the way, and we sailed past statues and all the quiet office blocks until we found the road that goes up to the dumpsite. We put Pia on the saddle, and the rest of us got off and pushed, running as fast as we could, so she was laughing too.

No police cars, nothing – but we still took no chances,

saying goodbye to the cycle boys finally, and creeping in sideways up the canal.

My first thing was the school – the Mission School. So I took a great handful of notes, put them down my shirt, and I did just what Gardo had told me we'd do. I skinned up the corner and was in through the bars. It seemed my good old friend Father Juilliard – you still hadn't fixed them, sir, I could still get through: maybe you were hoping I'd be back – I'm joking. I put the money on his desk and grabbed a pen. I put my name again, big and black – and next to that all I could think of was flowers, so that's why I drew you a bunch, fast as I could, bursting up and open. Then I had my next very brilliant idea which – who knows? – maybe saved our lives like all the other times. Gardo says all I do is brag and take credit – we all had good ideas all the time, but this one was genius, because how else would we have blended into the morning?

Why it hit me, I don't know – I guess all of us have to keep thinking ahead and looking out for danger, or maybe Gabriel and José were still with us even this far – maybe they'd been pushing that bike with us. Or maybe I just saw the cupboard, I don't know. The point was – this was Father Juilliard's office – there were cupboards full of odds and ends, and one of them was the crazy school uniform store.

Little shirts and shorts! They'd been donated to us

years before by some charity volunteer who thought all the kids ought to look the same, like proper schoolkids – but it never caught on. To make us feel like a real school, I imagine, this kind person had given about a hundred white shirts, and a hundred blue shorts and a hundred little dresses. There were packets and packets, little slippers too. There were backpacks – the kind kids put their schoolbooks in, but there was scarcely a book in the place! What are the kids here going to carry apart from trash? The backpacks had the charity name, big and bold, all over them so you'll never forget who's being so nice.

So I grabbed a load of everything, and pushed it out of the bars. Then I followed them down where they fell, and we didn't even need to speak – we knew where we were going.

First we opened up four of the backpacks and stuffed them with dollars. We stuffed them full and zipped them up.

Then we turned back to what was left, which was most of it, and we took off every paper band – the bands that keep hundreds bundled into ten thousands. They were blowing around already, so we got them in the sheet and the sack and bundled them up again. I tell you, the dumpsite was alive now, because of the wind. Dust and grit was blowing about, and little bits of trash were whirling. The plastic roofs were flapping too, and a bit of metal sheet was banging. There was a very little bit of light in the sky, way over by the dock cranes, but no one was about just yet – or nobody saw us. We probably had ten or fifteen minutes before dawn, before the ghosts had to say goodbye and slip away. So we hauled everything to my old home, to where the big broken belt – belt number fourteen – just points up at the sky doing nothing.

No, I did not go down to see my friends the rats! Pia stayed on the ground, looking up at us, with the clothes and the bags. Then I went up first with the rope end, and pulled on it. Gardo and Raphael came next, taking the weight, and I went up and up and up. The wind was just getting stronger, and my shirt was flapping – I felt like I was up on a ship because the whole belt-frame was moving. We got the first bundle up right to the top, right to the top, and I could see way over Behala, way over the city, way out to sea! Then Raphael came up next to me, crying out he was so happy – just shouting into the wind – and we held each other and howled. We took handfuls of the money then, and threw them up into the sky. The notes spilled out and whirled, and it was a storm of money. Typhoon Terese, I later heard, racing in from south China – and the next day the rains would burst. Right now, the wind got under all the cash we could throw, and pushed it up and out, and spun it right across the land.

Soon my arm was aching.

Raphael stopped shouting and just clung there, exhausted. We did the next bundle more slowly, and as it got lighter, Gardo came up too, right up to the top of the belt, and he had strong arms, and he helped us throw the rest. When Gardo came, the wind rose up even more, and we were clinging to that crane! It was a hurricane, and a hurricane of money. We must have thrown five and a half million dollars out over the dumpsite, and that wild wind took it all over the whole of our big, beautiful, terrible town.

At the bottom of it all, what did we find? We found another letter, slipped in with the cash. It was from José Angelico, so Gardo stuffed it down his shirt. We dropped the sheet. We slowly climbed down, and we were dizzy.

Pia was waiting for us by the rucksacks. She'd unwrapped the clothes, and put the plastic packets into a pile, and was sitting on them. We changed. We washed our faces by the school tap. Then we made our way out of Behala.

I wanted to watch. I wanted to hang back and see what happened when the first trash boy of the morning hooked up – not a stupp, but a hundred-dollar bill. Gardo was firm, though – and I'd come to see that you didn't cross Gardo, not to his face.

Raphael had goodbyes to say, and I could see him lingering. Then again, so did Gardo. In the end I think they knew it was easier to go without goodbyes – there was no choice – and I saw Gardo put his arm round Raph and lead him on.

He said we had a train to catch, so we went off and caught it.

6

Raphael, Gardo, Jun, Pia.

We are writing together for the last chapter.

Thank you, Father Juilliard and Sister Olivia. Thank you, Grace, and thank you, Mr Gonz, for helping us to tell our story. We are at the end, nearly where we started – just catching the train . . .

We caught it on the curve it makes south of Behala, where it slows down nice and safe. Yes, we were just three schoolboys and a little schoolgirl, in through the windows and onto the seats. There weren't many people on it at first, but at Central loads of kids got on, most of them dressed like us, and we bought our tickets with the last of our pesos.

Like those kids, we had our school bags. They carried books; we carried dollars. Soon they were getting down for their schools, and we just carried on.

It was a long way to Sampalo, but we always knew we'd get there. The train took us through the night, and put us, just before dawn, at the ferry port. We crossed over the sea for nine hours, to a little place called Fort Barton. Then we caught a bus to the eastern shore. We got a cycle rickshaw from there to the jetty, and another little boat took us way out, to where the water changes colour – to the deep turquoise you can see right through. It is paradise.

We stepped out at last onto a beach, and we started walking.

Yes. You walk far enough and the earth does turn to soft sand, and now we are in a place more beautiful than creation.

That was some time ago. We have since bought boats, and learned how to fish, and we can tell you the truth, for the lying is finished. We will fish for ever and live happy lives. That is our plan, and nothing will stop us.

THE END

Appendix

A letter from José Angelico:

To whom it may concern:

I am writing this knowing that if it is in another man's hands, then I am dead or soon to die. I took this money hoping that I would be the one to return it to where it belongs, and I had my schemes for doing that. But I write as a dead man, I think: for they will not take me and let me live.

My daughter is Pia Dante Angelico, and she has nobody in the world now. Perhaps I can appeal to you to make her safe and help her? She is as innocent as they are all innocent; I know I am betraying her. Pia, if ever you get to see this, know that my mission was simple, and what I did, I did for you and children like you. From the day I came to know Mr Gabriel Olondriz – and I was a very young boy when I met him – a fire burned.

He set me ablaze, as he started so many fires. He taught me many things, but he taught me most of all that Senator Zapanta's crime – the crime he uncovered and was jailed for – was monumental. Senator Zapanta stopped a nation in its tracks. He stopped our country making progress. Worse than that even, he gave other countries an excuse to stop helping us. For the millions he took, how many millions did he prevent even being offered? Worse, worse even than that – he reassured other politicians, officers, clerks, teachers, shopkeepers, neighbours that to steal is to rise, and to rise with your foot on the face of the poor is natural law. Even the poor believe that, and it is one of the reasons we stay poor.

Pia, I got tired waiting. There is a saying from St Matthew, 'Knock, and the door shall be opened' – and maybe that is true of God, but it is not true of man. The locks and chains that I have seen. The seals on the doors, my child. In our life, the doors remain shut. That is why I set my life to serving

Senator Zapanta, in the hope that one day he would leave his door ajar, and let me through it.

I waited many years before he did, so let me tell you what happened, just so there is no mystery. Just so you know how simple it can be, to rob those who rob us.

Senator Zapanta has a traditional, frightened mind. His smiles are false: he is worried all the time. He has lost money in bad deals, and he despises banks. His own father lost a lot of money when a bank collapsed: Senator Zapanta trusts only cash. That is why in the basement of his home he built a vault, and that is why the dirty money from his crimes is kept under the ground.

He moves money from the vault to a smaller safe upstairs. He only moves small sums, keeping the main chamber locked. It requires a key and a combination. How do I know this? Because he came to trust me with both. To live without trust is difficult, and tiring. What he came to trust in me,

Pia, was what he thought was my sweet, obedient stupidity. I have spent the years being only willing and obedient. I have followed orders, and smiled. I have spent a lifetime nodding, serving, providing, assisting – and no task has ever been too great, just as no task has ever been left undone. For those reasons, I rose and got closer. I became essential to Senator Zapanta, because I was one of the only men in whom he placed trust.

He took me down to the vault eight years ago. The door is metal, and so heavy it runs on wheels. Inside the room are locked boxes, but the cash was kept on a shelf, in bricks. Those bricks came and went. He told me he liked to have six million there, because six million filled the shelves. When the bricks of cash ran down, he would move money from his banks, and a briefcase would arrive. He started by always taking me down with him. Then – one day, three years ago – he gave me the key, and the combination, and sent me down alone. He would change the combination after every trip, of course – so there was never any danger of me visiting the vault without permission. I came to see that he only used five sets of numbers. He had five sons, so he used the birthdays of his boys. He thought I was too stupid to memorize numbers, and the key – he knew – could not be copied if it never left the house. He did not imagine that in my room I kept notes, and memorized them, and worked out the variations of numbers. Pia, I burned my notes in the kitchen stove lest anyone check. I learned from Gabriel Olondriz, and I burned them as soon as I made them.

He was right about the key, of course, but – once again – he did not think his houseboy would draw it and take the drawing to a locksmith on the other side of the city. He did not think the houseboy would return, and try the copy the next time he got a chance, and note how it failed to match, drawing revisions carefully and crumpling the paper to look like trash, to smuggle it out again. He never thought that, just like my godfather in jail, with years to think and plan – I, José Angelico, thought in years rather than days or hours. Sixteen times I tried the key-copies before we got it right. Then it was a question of waiting for the right combination of circumstances. When Senator Zapanta announced a three-month trip to Europe, it seemed the time. The house staff was scaled down. Repairs and re-decoration of several rooms was announced – this would mean so many visitors. I started to worry about the fridge in the servants' kitchen, and I broke the thermostat twice, and mended it again. When someone suggested we call in the repair man, I told my friends that I'd run out of patience and would buy a new one myself, out of my own wages. The housekeeper promised she would try to make it a house purchase, but I told her that in this hot country we needed a reliable fridge, and I would not wait.

The housekeeper trusted me. The guards trusted me. The thing I worried about most was that once I'd filled the fridge with money, we'd be stopped at the gate and searched – we are routinely searched, of course. But I was José Angelico, with the right papers, and there were delivery vehicles going in and out all morning, and I'd wrapped the thing in plastic and roped it ready for loading. We sailed through.

Getting the money from the vault to the fridge? It took two trips. I chose a Thursday, which is when I pull all the household trash together for the dump truck. Nobody is surprised to see the houseboy dragging two, three or four awkward bags of trash around – especially when the builders are at work, making so much mess. When Senator Zapanta discovers the simplicity with which six million dollars disappears, I hope that he will fall to his knees and howl. Remember, Pia – and remember, Senator – whatever is said about me, I was no thief. I simply took back the money that was ours, and now I am about to put it in this coffin.

I have, of course, created the alternative route: if you have travelled this route, it is only with the help of Mr Olondriz – so I hope you are a friend. My final letter to him will lie in box 101, for 101 is the thing you cannot resist. With it lie instructions that only he will understand. The key to the box will stay safe with me.

Now I am so tired.

I am about to place the coffin in a grave that will be marked with your name, my child. I mean to find a way of returning it to the people from whom it was stolen. But if someone is reading this, it means I am almost certainly dead and the money is in their hands, and I can only say, 'Beware, because this money belongs to the poor. That is what you cannot resist.'

It seems fitting that the Day of the Dead is approaching. We will meet again, Pia Dante, but in the brightest of lights.

It is accomplished.

A Note from the Author:
What is a book-code?

I first came across the device in a novel by John le Carré. It was explained as a very simple code that relied on two or more people having exactly the same copy of a book. For example, if I know that you have the Penguin 1975 edition of *Under the Volcano*, I can get my own copy out and communicate thus:

234.15.1.3.3.7.4.16.4/8.2.6.15.5.3.16.2.3.4.19.16.

The most important number is the first: it identifies the page. Now you're at that page, you count fifteen lines down. At line fifteen, you go just one letter in, which gives you a capital 'B'. Now go to line three, character three. It gives you an 'e'. On you plod and you end up with *Best*. You now hit an oblique stroke, which means you go onto the next page. Eight lines down and two characters in give you 'w', and soon you have 'wishes'.

So oblique strokes signify the turning of the page and the creation of a new word. Counting characters left to right must include spaces and punctuation marks. To avoid confusion, indented lines can be avoided – but there are endless variations, and you can personalize the rules to your own satisfaction, making things as complex as you wish. The joy of a book-code is that you can make it entirely your own.

The code can be cracked if you know the book the messengers are using, but it's impossible if you don't. The code used by José Angelico is revealed if you have the 1984 New King James Thomas Nelson edition of the Bible. Gabriel Olondriz had a copy, and those wishing to send him secret messages had copies too. They had personalized the code, working right to left, and turning pages backwards rather than forwards. I presume the messages exchanged were never of great importance, and it was done simply for the joy of encryption. But it was how José concealed the most important part of his trail, and he invoked his God at the same time.

940,4,18,13,14,/5,3,6,4,/9,1,12,10,3,3,/12,9,2,3,25,32,/
6,1,6,2,1,11,/3,3,3,2,1,6,15,5,1,6/5,11,1,6,/2,4,5,2,5,4,/3,1,4,1,4,1
,13,28/2,16,4,7,7,1,/5,9,11,2,5,6,/2,7,6,2,7,2,21,7,7,3,7,5,1,2,1,1,
7,5,/16,3,7,9,12,6,4,3,5,1,/1,4,11,3,/2,6,3,1,1,2,1,9,1,4,

Author Acknowledgements

I am eternally grateful to Jane Turnbull and Joe, without whom I would not be in print. I am grateful to my own family and to a number of close friends, most especially Jane Fisher for her support, and Michael Hemsley, who gave me the idea that sparked the plot.

I wrote this book whilst teaching the children of British School Manila – a truly fine school that offers what every child is entitled to, but so few receive – and I thank them, as well as my colleagues, for their kindness.

I would also like to thank Linda, Hannah, Bella and David at David Fickling Books, as well as Clare and the whole Random House team. Ken, Sally and Jenne have also been – and continue to be – dynamic.

Behala dumpsite is based loosely on a place I visited whilst living in Manila. There really is a school there, and there really are children who will crawl through trash forever. If you come to the Philippines, do what Olivia did. See everything, and fall in love.

The characters and the plot are, of course, invented.